EXPULSION

To my parents, Jean and Michael

EXPULSION
ENGLAND'S JEWISH
SOLUTION

RICHARD HUSCROFT

TEMPUS

Cover Illustration Credits

Front: Jews wearing the tabula being driven out of England in 1290, from an early
fourteenth-century chronicle. Courtesy of the British Library, Cotton Nero D.II f.183v.
Thirteenth-century drawing of London from the margin of a manuscript of Geoffrey of
Monmouth's *History of the Kings of Britain*. Courtesy of Jonathan Reeve, JR350b18p159
12001300.
Back: The Jew, Aaron of Colchester. Courtesy of Jonathan Reeve, JR760b11p393
12501300. The multi-faced wheeler-dealer Isaac of Norwich, crowned in mockery in a
record of 1233. Courtesy of Jonathan Reeve, JR330b11p392 12001300.

First published 2006

Tempus Publishing Limited
The Mill, Brimscombe Port,
Stroud, Gloucestershire, GL5 2QG
www.tempus-publishing.com

© Richard Huscroft, 2006

British Library Cataloguing in Publication Data.
A catalogue record for this book is available from the British Library.

ISBN 0 7524 3729 1

Typesetting and origination by Tempus Publishing Limited
Printed in Great Britain

Contents

About the Author

Richard Huscroft is a History Master at Westminster School, London. He graduated from Oxford University with a First in History and was awarded his PhD from King's College London. His other books include *Ruling England 1042–1217*. He lives in London.

Acknowledgements

It will soon become clear how much this book owes to the work of other scholars. I hope that some of my own ideas are apparent amongst theirs, but the former are far outnumbered by the latter. I would also like to thank Jonathan Reeve for offering me the chance to write the book in the first place, and David Carpenter for reading through my first draft with characteristic incisiveness and generosity. Jo and Matilda have provided me with the time and inspiration to complete it. Finally, the dedication is a quite inadequate token of my love and gratitude for a lifetime of selfless support.

A Note on Money

During the period covered by this book, there was only one coin in circulation in England, the silver penny. There were twelve pence in a shilling, 240 pence (twenty shillings) in a pound and 160 pence in a mark. A mark, therefore, was equivalent to two-thirds of a pound. However, shillings, pounds and marks were terms used for accounting purposes only; there were no coins with those values. As far as Jewish affairs are concerned, many of their financial dealings, either with their own clients or with the royal government, were expressed in marks. Throughout this book, however, and for the sake of simplicity and ready comparability, I have converted all sums originally expressed in marks into pounds. Thus, for example, a tallage of 1,000 marks would be referred to here as one of £666 13s 4d, or, in other words, £666, thirteen shillings and four pence.

Abbreviations

Full citations for all of the following works are given in the Select Bibliography.

Ann. Dunstable	*Annales Prioratus de Dunstaplia, A.D. 1–1377,* ed. Luard in *Ann. Mon.*, iii
Ann. London	*Annales Londonienses,* ed. Stubbs in *Chronicles of the Reigns of Edward I and Edward II,* i
Ann. Mon.	*Annales Monastici,* ed. Luard
Ann. Osney	*Annales Monasterii de Oseneia, 1016–1347,* ed. Luard in *Ann. Mon.*, iv
Ann. Waverley	*Annales Monasterii de Waverleia, A.D. 1–1291,* ed. Luard in *Ann. Mon.*, ii
Cal. Ch. R.	*Calendar of Charter Rolls*
CCR	*Calendar of Close Rolls*
Close Rolls	*Close Rolls of the Reign of Henry III*
Cotton	*Bartholomaei de Cotton, Historia Anglicana (A.D. 449–1298),* ed. Luard
CPR	*Calendar of Patent Rolls*

CPREJ	*Calendar of the Plea Rolls of the Exchequer of the Jews*
EHD	*English Historical Documents*
EHR	*English Historical Review*
Foedera	*Foedera, Conventiones, Litterae, et Acta Publica*, I, ed. Rymer
Guisborough	*The Chronicle of Walter of Guisborough*, ed. Rothwell
JHS	*Jewish Historical Studies*
JJS	*Journal of Jewish Studies*
Liber	*Liber de Antiquis Legibus: Cronica maiorum et vicecomitum Londoniarum*, ed. Stapleton
ODNB	*Oxford Dictionary of National Biography*, ed. Matthew and Harrison
Oxenedes	*Chronica Johannis de Oxenedes*, ed. Ellis
PR	*Pipe Roll*
Rigg, *Select Pleas*	*Select Pleas, Starrs and other Records from the Rolls of the Exchequer of the Jews 1220-1284*, ed. Rigg
Rot. Chart.	*Rotuli Chartarum, 1199-1216*, ed. Hardy
Rot. Litt. Claus.	*Rotuli Litterarum Clausarum in Turri Londiniensi asservati*, ed. Hardy
Rot. Litt. Pat.	*Rotuli Litterarum Patentium in Turri Londiniensi asservati*, ed. Hardy
Rot. Oblat.	*Rotuli de Oblatis et Finibus in Turri Londiniensi asservati*, ed. Hardy
RS	*Rolls Series*
TCE	*Thirteenth Century England*, ed. Coss, Lloyd et al
TJHSE	*Transactions of the Jewish Historical Society of England*
Wykes	*Chronicon vulgo dictum Chronicon Thomae Wykes, 1066–1289*, ed. Luard in *Ann. Mon.*, iv

Introduction

William of Normandy's victory at the battle of Hastings in October 1066 and the subsequent conquest of England by him, his followers and his successors rightly occupy places of central importance in the history of Britain. Less well known is the fact that the Normans were not the only group of immigrants to cross the English Channel from northern France in the years after William's triumph. Some time between 1066 and 1100, a Jewish community was established in England (perhaps the first ever, although there may have been Jews in Roman Britain), probably at London, and in the following century other such settlements were founded across the kingdom. In 1290, however, only 200 years or so after they had arrived there, the Jews were expelled from England by King Edward I, and it would be over 350 years before they were permitted to return. So although there were almost certainly individual Jews in England at times both before and after these two dates, 1066 and 1290 effectively mark the beginning and end of the Jewish presence in medieval England.

Even during these two centuries, England's Jews were never numerically significant, but they played an important role in the life of the kingdom and a study of that role is crucial to an understanding of the social, religious, economic and political history of the period. The Jews of medieval England also played an important part in the wider history of their people. Not only was the English Expulsion of 1290 the first event of its kind to take place on such a comprehensive and conclusive scale; but it was also in England that the myth of the Jewish 'blood libel' was born in the middle of the twelfth century. Because of these events, and because of the ignorance and credulity which produced them, much misery has been caused.

One aim of this book is therefore to provide a brief and, I hope, clear account of this vital part of English, European and Jewish history. I have tried to explain the context within which England's Jews lived, worked and survived between the Conquest and the Expulsion. And in particular I have tried to analyse the reasons why medieval England's Jewish minority was treated as it was and why it was eventually banished from the kingdom. I have done this with some qualms and reservations, however. First, in the light of what happened to the Jews during the twentieth century, and also in the light of their continuing struggle to secure recognition and acceptance in the face of persistent, widespread anti-Semitism and hostility, the study of any aspect of Jewish history is bound to be problematic; arguments and their emphases will inevitably be loaded with more layers of meaning and significance than less controversial subjects usually bear. Colin Richmond has most recently given a powerful reminder of how precise and careful historians' language about the Jews needs to be if it is not to lend support to ancient prejudices and bigoted stereotypes.[1] Second, I am neither Jewish nor a specialist in Jewish history, and others are much better qualified than I to write a comprehensive and fully detailed history of medieval

English Jewry. Consequently, this book is not designed to be an exhaustive analysis of its subject, merely an introduction to it. Third, this book sees the history of England's medieval Jews very much as the history of their relationship with the English king and his government. Where possible, I have tried to bring forward examples of how England's Jews related to each other and to the wider Christian world around them, and in Chapter 3 in particular I have dwelt on this a little more. Nevertheless, the bulk of the available evidence and the greater part of the research which has been carried out to date tend to force any analysis of this kind down those official channels where the records are most plentiful. Despite the problems of interpretation, however, and despite its limitations, I hope this book will still provide a useful and digestible entry into a subject of essential relevance and abiding interest.

Before the main themes of this book come into focus, though, it is probably helpful to think a little more about who the Jews who came to England after 1066 actually were, and to consider what has been written about them already. Again, I can do little more than scratch the surface of these huge subjects. In medieval Christendom, however, few would have disputed that the Jews were God's 'chosen people'. They were believed to be the descendants of Abraham, who had come to Canaan (later known as Palestine and now Israel) from Mesopotamia, of his son Isaac and of his grandson Jacob, or Israel. According to the biblical narrative, God had said to Abraham, 'I will make you into a great nation and I will bless you... and all peoples on earth will be blessed by you'.[2] But it was Moses, the first and greatest of all the prophets, who is traditionally considered to have been the real founder of the Jewish religion and the unifier of its different peoples or tribes. Moses led these tribes out of their slavish captivity in Egypt under the Pharaohs (they had taken refuge there initially to escape famine in Palestine); he kept them together during forty years in the wilderness and brought them to the borders of the Promised Land before he died aged 120. Moses also gave his people a set of laws which had been revealed to him on Mount Sinai by the one true God, and a set of moral and ethical standards by which many modern Jews still aspire to live. This Law (the Torah) is found in the first five books of the Bible (the Pentateuch), and it governs everything from civil law to diet and personal hygiene. It provides the essential tenets of a religious system as well as a code of social conduct and organisation.

Whether Abraham or Moses were real people is of course open to serious question. The events with which they are associated, if anything like them took place at all, may have happened in about 1800 and 1200 BCE respectively. And whether the Jewish belief in a single God emerged suddenly or gradually over time is equally obscure. It does seem clearer, however, that a particular kinship group, the *bene* Jacob (descendants of Jacob), gradually ceased to be nomadic and settled in areas of Canaan. Different parts of this group followed different histories, but as they began to settle, so they began more formally to unite in the defence, and then conquest, of territory, making a covenant, not only with each other, but also under the demand and protection of Yhwh, the four letters of the Hebrew name for God, which traditionally is never pronounced. Under David in about 1000 BCE, the biblical narrative continues, Jerusalem was captured, and there the Temple was built by Solomon. About 597 BCE and again *c.* 586 BCE, however, the city was devastated by Nebuchadnezzar, and many of its inhabitants were deported to Babylon. The return from the Exile was followed, after some years, by the rebuilding of the Temple in 520–515 BCE. There Judaism was consolidated as a religion based on the Bible, and Jews began to separate themselves clearly from non-Jews by rituals (most importantly, circumcision), by the observance of the Sabbath and the recognition of the Law. There was further persecution in the second century BCE, however, when Jerusalem was sacked by the forces of King Antiochus of Syria. Peace was made, and the Temple, which was by now the centre of the Jewish faith, was cleansed by Judas Maccabeus in 165 BCE. This event is still commemorated today in the annual Festival of Lights or Hannukah. But a century or so later, with the Roman annexation of Palestine by Pompey in 63 BCE, the Jews there had new overlords. This was the situation as the Christian era dawned.

According to the traditional Jewish view of events, at some time in the first century CE a Jew called Jesus set up a new religion which borrowed significantly from Judaism, but which also departed markedly and, the Jews thought, erroneously from tradition when his followers began to claim that Jesus was not just a prophet but the Messiah, the son of God himself. The parallel Christian view also acknowledged the ancient credentials of Judaism. But Jesus was the son of God, Christians insisted, and it was his achievement to bring the old religion to its perfect, culminated state. The Jews were simply in error in refusing to accept this. So for medieval Jews and Christians, there was no doubt that the two religions had common origins; Jesus would have thought of himself as a Jew, after all. After his death, however, differences between more mainstream Judaism and the small Jewish sect which the followers of Jesus established began to harden. One of their leaders, Paul, who had previously campaigned energetically against the followers of Jesus, but who had been converted dramatically to their cause, wanted to make it easy for non-Jews (or Gentiles) to convert to the new religion – they need not be circumcised or subscribe to the Law, he argued. But this was too much for traditional Jews who viewed such matters as central to the way their identity as a community and as a people was defined.

The Jews were not helped at this crucial point by political developments either. In first-century Palestine, like the fledgling Christians, they were imperial subjects and open to exploitation. In 66 CE, inspired to an extent by their belief that a Messiah would come to help restore the Jewish kingdom, the Jews rose in violent revolt against their Roman occupiers, but in 70 CE, after initial successes for the rebels, Jerusalem was taken by the Romans, the revolt was brutally crushed and the Temple was destroyed, a decisive event in the history of the Jewish people. With its hereditary priesthood, daily rituals and annual celebrations involving animal and non-animal sacrifices, the Temple had become the centre of Jewish religious life. After 70 CE, and after a further unsuccessful revolt against the Romans in 132–5 CE, the Jews no longer possessed their own holy lands and places. As a result, those scattered Jewish communities or 'diaspora' which by this time existed outside the biblical Promised Land, in Babylon, Greece, Rome, Asia Minor and elsewhere, were now deprived of the unifying influence provided by the Temple and the city of Jerusalem. The local synagogue became the place for public worship, teaching and study, and the family took its place at the centre of Jewish life. At the same time, wider authority within these communities started to become concentrated in the hands of the rabbis, originally honoured teachers to whom this title was given.

Rabbinic Judaism, with its classic written text, the Talmud, eventually spread to most of the Jewish world, but after Christianity was made the official religion of the Roman Empire by Constantine in the early fourth century, life for Jews became even more precarious as the views of the Christian Church about them were formed and began to harden. The Jews continued to act as a distinct and exclusive religious and racial minority; they ate different food and obeyed different laws. They were wrong about Jesus, too, the theory went. But what made all of these things appear worse was the role allegedly played by the Jews in Christ's death. By the fifth century, the standard Christian position was that the Jews were collectively responsible for deicide. By not accepting Jesus and by refusing to save him when they had had the chance to do so, the Jews had effectively killed him. With the might of the Roman administrative machine behind such beliefs, moreover, the Jews soon came to be treated as second-class citizens, excluded as they were from political and military functions, forbidden to marry Christians, make wills or give evidence in courts of law.

With the collapse of the Roman Empire and the rise of Islam, however, the position of the Jews changed once again. The spectacular Muslim conquests of Byzantium, Syria, Palestine, North Africa and Spain in the seventh and eighth centuries brought many Jews under Muslim rule. In Spain in particular, they prospered and shared in the great achievements made there in the fields of astronomy, philosophy and mathematics. It was here that the type of Judaism known as 'Sephardic' developed. In the rest of Europe, where 'Ashkenazic' Jewry was established, the treatment they experienced varied. The early Carolingian rulers used Jews as settlers and soldiers, and encouraged them to trade. But although secular rulers appreciated their usefulness and value, the attitude of the Church to the Jews in these lands always meant that they would find life difficult. As will be seen, the fear that good Christian men, women and children would be corrupted and their souls endangered if they had too much contact with Jews was a persistent and stubborn one throughout the medieval period. Nevertheless, by the end of the tenth century, Jewish communities were established in several places in northern France. The power of the Carolingian kings had long since collapsed, but at urban centres such as Paris, Le Mans, Orléans and Rouen, Jews were managing to live and trade. To do so, however, and in the absence of strong, centralised authority, they were forced to rely on local rulers for protection and security. One such ruler, albeit one more powerful than most, was the duke of Normandy, whose chief city was Rouen. It is at this point that the story of England's medieval Jews really begins.

Traditionally, however, interest in England's medieval Jews amongst historians has been limited. In 1738, De Bloissiers Tovey published his *Anglia Judaica*, the first comprehensive history of the Jewish experience in England. Thereafter, however, it was to be another century and a half before England's Jewish history attracted the attention of serious, determined scholars once again. At the end of the nineteenth century and during the first half of the twentieth, inspired and invigorated by the Anglo-Jewish Historical Exhibition of 1887 and the foundation of the Jewish Historical Society in 1894, the works of, amongst others, Joseph Jacobs, Lionel Abrahams, Mayer Domnitz Davis and Michael Adler gave Anglo-Jewish history a multiplicity of authoritative voices and newly published sources at a time when anti-Semitism was still commonplace and when work in this field was, if not frowned upon, then treated lightly in wider academic circles. It was still not viewed as an essential component in the study of British medieval history (arguably it is still struggling to be so), but in the mid-twentieth century the works of Peter Elman, and a little later those of Vivian Lipman, went a considerable way towards forcibly correcting this unbalanced approach by demanding to be noticed. It was the remarkable work of Cecil Roth, however, which set the standard for the future. His *A History of the Jews in England* was first published in 1941 when the condition of European Jewry was under threat like never before. It is the most important and outstanding of the many contributions Roth made to the study of Anglo-Jewish history, and in its thoroughness, insight and its trailblazing courage probably the most significant of all works published on the subject. It still has much to offer, and its influence on the present work will be obvious throughout.

By the time Roth wrote his *History*, moreover, the resources and materials available to the student of medieval England's Jews had expanded significantly. By the middle of the twentieth century, many of the most important records of post-Conquest English central government, including many of the pipe rolls of the royal Exchequer and the letter rolls of the royal Chancery, which contain huge amounts of information of Jewish interest, had been published, not least as a result of the efforts of Jacobs, Abrahams and Davis. What remains, thanks to organisations such as the Pipe Roll Society, continues to be produced today. And specifically dealing with Jewish affairs in the thirteenth century were the records of the Exchequer of the Jews, the separate government department set up in the late twelfth century to deal with the business of the king's Jewish subjects. Most of these have now been published for the period prior to the Expulsion. This ever-increasing mountain of information was utilised most effectively by Henry Richardson, who produced his seminal *English Jewry under Angevin Kings* in 1960. So influential was this wide-ranging work, which is still in many ways the starting point for students of all aspects of medieval English Jewry, that Roth felt compelled to produce a heavily revised third edition of his own *History* in 1964. Together, these two books continue to act as benchmarks and inspiring examples of what is possible for writers of Anglo-Jewish medieval history, although the concerns of Roth's work, of course, extended well beyond the medieval period.

During the 1970s, however, the results of further research into medieval Anglo-Jewish history were published only intermittently. Some of this work, Barrie Dobson's on the York Jewry, for example, Gavin Langmuir's on Little St Hugh and Paul Hyams' on the Jewish minority as a whole, was ground-breaking, but it was still isolated and exposed on the colder fringes of mainstream historical writing on medieval

England. Since the 1980s, however, attitudes have begun to change. As the fields of study in social, cultural and gender history have expanded, so interest in English medieval Jewry has developed, too. The pioneers of the 1970s have continued to produce important work, but they have been joined over the last twenty years or so by a new group of prolific scholars, most notably Robert Stacey, Joe Hillaby, Zefirah Rokeah and Robin Mundill. Between them they have cast an extraordinary amount of fresh light on the relationship between the king and the Jews, on the histories of individual Jewish communities, on the commercial activities of individual Jews and their clients, on the Expulsion itself and on many other areas. More recently still, the scope for opening up new avenues of investigation has been revealed by, for example, Suzanne Bartlet's work on the lives and careers of Jewish women in medieval England. Interest in all aspects of medieval Anglo-Jewish history has perhaps never been greater; no student of the wider history of England in the Middle Ages can now afford to ignore it. Unfortunately, though, the endeavours of those working on this subject are still best known only in specialist circles, and the results of their research have tended to be published only in academic journals which are often obscure and hard to find. They deserve to reach a wider audience, and I hope this book will go some way towards furthering this process.

1

The Jews in Anglo-Norman England 1066–1154

B y the end of the first Christian millennium, Jewish communities were established in many parts of Europe. The oldest of these were in the south, in Italy, southern France and northern Spain. Of more recent origin, although many were still of long standing by 1000, were those communities north of the river Loire, which together formed what is often referred to as 'Ashkenazic' Jewry, and of which medieval English Jewry, the subject of this book, was a branch. Evidence concerning these centres of Jewish population before the end of the eleventh century is patchy and very limited; and only occasionally do particular communities or individuals emerge from the records. In the 1060s, for example, Christian warriors en route to Spain to fight the Muslim powers there attacked several Jewish communities they encountered. Their behaviour provoked a strong rebuke from Pope Alexander II.[1] And before this, between 1007 and 1012, a series of pronouncements was issued by governments across Europe offering Jews the choice between conversion to Christianity and expulsion, or death. There were massacres of Jews at Orléans, Rouen, Limoges, in the Rhineland and at Rome.[2] Why such a vicious anti-Jewish reaction occurred at this time is unclear, although fears concerning the spread of heresy and the significance of the Millennium may have played their part. Christians in the High Middle Ages believed that the end of the world was imminent, and the thousandth anniversary either of Christ's birth (in 1000) or of his death (in 1033) seemed a likely time for such momentous events. Mankind was living, it was thought, at the end of time, and the conversion of the Jews was seen as an essential precondition of Christ's Second Coming. Moreover, what these massacres, fifty years or so apart, had in common was the spurious link increasingly being made in the Christian imagination between the perceived evils of Islam and Judaism. This was obvious in the 1060s where the Jews were seen as 'infidels' equivalent to the Muslims and therefore just as deserving of slaughter. And the events of *c.*1010 may have come about in part as a result of rumours that the Jews had persuaded their Muslim allies to destroy the Holy Sepulchre, the site of Christ's burial, in Jerusalem. This conflation of Jews and Muslims as effectively interchangeable 'enemies of Christ' was a sign of worse things to come for European Jewry.

Relatively untouched by such fervour and bigotry, however, were the British Isles; and in particular their largest and most powerful constituent part, the kingdom of England. It is impossible to be sure when the first Jewish community settled in England. However, what evidence there is suggests that none was established until after 1066. This does not mean, of course, that Jews were unknown to the English before the Norman Conquest. Travellers and pilgrims from England would have encountered Jews abroad, and Jewish traders and merchants from northern France and Germany almost certainly visited Roman and Anglo-Saxon England. An awareness of the Jewish people, their customs and their history would also have developed as Christianity took an ever firmer hold on England from the seventh century onwards. Inevitably, too, as knowledge of the Old and New Testaments deepened, and as Christian views on the Jews hardened, prejudice against them is likely to have intensified in England just as it did on the continent. It has been pointed out, for example, how anti-Jewish rhetoric can be found in English royal documents of the tenth century. And it has been suggested that Jews were excluded from Anglo-Saxon England by royal order.[3] This would certainly account for their otherwise rather mysterious absence from the Old English kingdom. However, it remains impossible to know just how much was really known in England about Jewish beliefs and practices when the first Jewish settlers crossed the English Channel at some point during the last third of the eleventh century. But it is probably right to say that, because there had been no settled Jewish presence in England before 1066, when they did arrive in the kingdom the Jews were 'aliens in medieval England to a more profound degree than perhaps anywhere else in western Europe'.[4]

Just as there can be no certainty about precisely when these first settlers arrived in England, so it is also impossible to know how many of them made the trip. However, it is generally thought that they came from Normandy, and that they came because the ruler of Normandy, Duke William, who had become king of England after his victory over Harold II at Hastings in October 1066, had invited – probably even ordered – them to come. There is nothing from William's reign to show that the Jewish plantation in England was his idea, but at least one twelfth-century writer, William of Malmesbury, thought that the king was responsible for their importation.[5] Duke William, after all, was accustomed to having Jews settled within his territories; there was a well-established and prosperous Jewish community at Rouen, William's chief city, by the eleventh century. However, he would not have brought them to England simply as a comforting reminder of home. Financial imperatives almost certainly lay behind the new king's decision. Although not all Jews by any means made their livings from such activities, they had acquired a reputation by the late eleventh century as traders in luxury goods, moneychangers and dealers in plate and coin. And it has been suggested that the Jews of eleventh-century Rouen allowed the rulers of Normandy sustained and profitable access to German silver and to the luxury goods markets of North Africa and the Mediterranean.[6]

It is worth emphasising that the establishment of Jewish settlement in England after 1066 was not a unique phenomenon at this time, and that it fitted into a series of more general trends. Eleventh-century Europe was a dynamic place. The frontiers of Western Christendom were being extended by aggressive, expansionist rulers in Muslim Spain and southern Italy. Others, and William the Conqueror is the prime example, were adding to their territories by conquering the lands of fellow Christian rulers.[7] In this way England (although hardly a backwater before 1066) was brought more into the mainstream of prevailing European political, economic and cultural trends than ever before. There was population growth across Europe, too, from the late tenth century onwards; and with that came migration and an increase in the amount of land under cultivation. But whilst the vast majority of Europe's people continued to live and work on the land, urbanisation was also a characteristic of this period, and the number of settlements which can reasonably be described as 'towns' began to grow across Europe. Towns were centres of trade and commerce; as their number grew, so too probably did the amount of money in circulation.[8] Consequently, great profits were to be derived from these new urban settlements and the rulers of territories were understandably keen to control them as much as they could. In Germany in 1084, for example, after a catastrophic fire in the Jewish neighbourhood in Mainz, the bishop of Speyer invited some of the survivors to resettle in his town. He did this, it has been suggested, not out of charity or pity, but because the bishop 'perceived the Jews as useful contributors to [his] effort at urban development'.[9] It is very likely that William the Conqueror saw the Jews he knew from Normandy in the same way. And in England after 1066, he would have expected them to play their part in ensuring that his new kingdom maximised its fabled wealth.

Clear evidence of the presence of Jews in England before the end of the eleventh century is scanty. But it was perhaps William II's reign (1087–1100) which saw the first expansion of the fledgling Jewish community there. After William I had first encouraged it, Jewish migration across the Channel may have been further stimulated by the violent persecution suffered by Jews at Rouen in the opening stages of the First Crusade in the mid-1090s, for example. Certainly, a doctrinal debate between Gilbert Crispin, Abbot of Westminster and Jacob, a French Jew educated in Germany, had taken place in England by early 1093. And William of Malmesbury, writing in the 1120s and 1130s, told the story of what had happened when representatives of London's Jewish community appeared before William II to present him with gifts on a religious festival. The irreverent king insisted that the Jews take part in a religious debate with members of his own clergy; if the Jews won, he said, 'he would become one of their sect'.[10] The primary purpose of such a tale was to demonstrate the king's scandalously flippant attitude to religion, and it would be unwise to give it too much credence; however, at least it clearly suggests that the London Jewry had been established in some form by the end of the eleventh century. The first clear reference to the Jewry there dates only from *c.*1127–8, however, when 'the street [*vicus*] of the Jews' was mentioned in a survey of properties belonging to the Dean and Chapter of St Paul's Cathedral. This street, it seems, was in one or another of the two

streets known today as Old Jewry ('Colechurch Lane' prior to
1290) and Ironmonger Lane.[11]

Within another thirty years or so, the Jews of London formed
an extremely wealthy community. Just how wealthy can be
gauged from perhaps the single most important English royal
record of the twelfth century, the pipe roll of 1130. Every year
at Michaelmas, the sheriffs of all the English counties, as well
as others who owed money to the king, appeared at the royal
Exchequer to have their accounts audited by the king's officials. Details of the audits for each county were recorded on
parchment, and the individual records were then sewn together
and rolled up; each roll thus resembled a large pipe, and hence
'pipe roll'. The roll for the financial year 1129–30 is the only
one which survives from Henry I's reign, but they survive in
a continuous series from 1156. They set out in great detail the
amounts of money paid into the royal coffers by the sheriffs and
the amounts owed to the king from a whole range of sources,
including the Jews. In 1129–30, the Jews of London were fined
£2,000 'for killing a sick man'; £600, the record further states,
was paid immediately. Such an entry is notable for various reasons.
Firstly, this was a gigantic sum considering that, during the second
half of the twelfth century, the average annual baronial income
in England was approximately £200.[12] Secondly, it shows how
much disposable income the Jews had, and how easy, and perhaps
tempting, it was for the king at least occasionally to extract such
large amounts from them. Certainly, a penalty of £2,000 for the
death of a single man seems disproportionate, and it is quite possible that the charge was a fantastic one, deliberately trumped up
as an excuse to milk the Jews of their wealth. Thirdly, it suggests
that London's Jews were involved in providing medical care. This
was a line of business they had traditionally been associated with
on the continent; King Henry I's own physician, indeed, Petrus
Alfonsi, was a converted Jew.[13] The roll of 1130 also demonstrates
other aspects of Jewish life in London at this time, as well as

other ways in which the king benefited from his relationship with London's Jews. The leader of the London community in 1130 appears to have been one 'Rubi Gotsce' or Rabbi Josce. He held property in London and Rouen; he was the founder of a dynasty of major Jewish financiers; and it has been suggested that he founded the *magnam scolam Iudeorum*, or Great Synagogue, on the eastern side of Colechurch Lane in London.[14] He was also one of a number of important Jewish businessmen who, the pipe roll reveals, lent money to the king himself. Payments by the king to individual Jews (£120 to Rabbi Josce and nearly £60 to 'Manasser', for example) were probably loan repayments. And several entries record how the king was paid for the help he gave to Jews who were trying to recover debts owed to them. One group of Jewish lenders offered the king ten gold marks (£60) for his help in their claim against Ranulf, Earl of Chester. And another group offered six gold marks for royal assistance in their action against Richard FitzGilbert.[15] Men such as Ranulf and Richard were members of England's political élite. However, the costs of maintaining themselves in an appropriate style were oner-ous and ongoing – households had to be funded, fine clothes had to be bought and castles needed to be built and repaired. The Jews provided a ready source of credit, and, for his part, it is likely that the king was quite happy to see his barons overstretch themselves in this way (Ranulf of Chester owed the king £2,000 in 1131, for example). Since he controlled the Jews (more will be said about this later), the king had the power to intervene in individual cases and either enforce or relax the creditors' demands. Thus Jewish debt could be used as a form of patronage by the king, and as a way of controlling potentially troublesome individuals. It is strik-ing, for example, that Richard FitzGilbert is also recorded on the 1130 pipe roll as having offered the king £133 6s 8d for his help in his dispute with the Jews of London.[16]

So where did the London Jewry get its income from? Clearly, they were lending money on a significant scale by 1130, and they would also have dealt in silver bullion and foreign coin, as well as in luxury goods such as furs and jewellery. However, at this stage, it has been suggested that 'their most profitable business was probably in plate' rather than lending.[17] There is little if any direct evidence for this, although there may be a hint of such activity in Henry I's purchase, at a cost of £10 5s 10d, of two silver cups from a London Jew called Abraham in 1129–30.[18] Nevertheless, there are certainly good reasons for assuming that such transactions took place on a far more extensive scale than the surviving evidence reveals.[19]

Now there is little doubt that London's Jews profited as much as they did in large part because of their special relationship with the English kings. The king's interest in encouraging trade and his need for funds helped foster this relationship, but it was founded ultimately on the fact that the Jews, who refused to accept the divinity of Jesus, formed a non-Christian minority wherever they lived in western Europe. The dominant Christian orthodoxy, based principally on the teachings of St Augustine, held that the Jews were fundamentally in error about the nature of God's plan for the world. The Jews' wait for a Messiah was fruitless, Christians believed, because the one true Messiah had already been, gone and promised to return. In contemporary images, therefore, Jews were often depicted as blind, to represent the fact they were unable to 'see' the truth; and the synagogue was often personified as a blindfolded figure. It was not just that the Jews had failed to interpret the scriptures properly, however. They were seen as the betrayers and deserters of Christ; they had had the chance to accept him, and they had failed to do so. More than this, by their actions they had condemned him to death. Despite this, the official position of the Christian Church with regard to the Jews was that, whilst their beliefs were misguided and wrong, they were to be tolerated and permitted to practise their faith. After all, they were the people of the Old Testament and had played a part in spreading God's word. At the same time, their activities were to be severely circumscribed and controlled in order to prevent them spreading their beliefs or influencing others. Put another way, Christians needed to be protected from the dangerous poison of Jewish beliefs; nevertheless, Jews should not be persecuted because their presence in Christian society was a reminder of Christ's Passion, and their eventual conversion was required as a sign of the Second Coming. The first authoritative collection of Church, or 'canon', law was compiled by the monk Gratian at Bologna in northern Italy in the 1140s. At various points in his collection, known as the *Decretum*, Gratian touched on the position of Jews. Thus, citing a letter of Pope Gregory the Great (590–604) and a decree of the Fourth Council of Toledo (633), he confirmed that Jews were not to be forcibly converted. Rather they should be persuaded to accept the truth of Christianity 'by gentle means rather than by harsh means lest adversity alienate the mind of those whom a reasonable argument would have been able to attract'. Gratian later went on to cite authority for the views that Jews should not marry Christians or own Christian slaves and that they should not occupy public office. More generally, Christians should not dine or live with Jews; nor should they accept medical treatment from them, or have any Jews as friends.

In ways such as these, the Church tried to keep Christians and Jews separate and apart. Ultimately, the goal was to convert them by persuasion. Nevertheless, they continued to be a focus for hostility and, regardless of the official position of the Church, Jews across Europe remained liable to persecution and very much an alien part of the dominant Christian community. Thus they needed protection if they were to carry on their lives and trading activities in peace, and after 1066 in England, it was the kings and their officers, principally the sheriffs and the custodians of the king's castles, who provided the protection they required. It is no coincidence that, within the towns where they settled, the Jewish quarters tended to be found near the local

castle. This was the seat of local power, and a convenient refuge in
time of persecution. The London Jewry was close to the Tower
of London, for example, and certainly by the thirteenth century
the constable of the Tower was exercising a policing jurisdiction
within the London Jewry. He may have done this during the
twelfth century, too.[20] In an emergency, of course, Jews would
take refuge wherever they could. During the great revolt of
1173-4 against Henry II, for example, the Jewish women and
children of Bury St Edmunds sheltered in the abbey where
the sacrist, William, was known as 'the father and patron of the
Jews'.[21] Thus, 'it was for reasons of security, self-preservation and
social welfare as well as the preservation of their religion that
they tended to live in centres which had a royal representative
or a powerful protector close at hand'.[22] This is not the whole
story, of course. Castles often contained the local mint and they
were regularly the place near to which royally authorised and
supervised fairs were held. Indeed, there is a clear correlation
between the places where Jews are known to have settled in the
first half of the twelfth century and the location of royal mints
and markets. The Bristol Jewry, for example, was near the top
of Broad Street and close to both the quay and the Guildhall.
And the Norwich Jewry was close to the Haymarket, the sheep
market and the wheat market.[23] There thus tended to be a convenient coincidence between the Jews' need for security and
their desire to carry on their commercial activities.

  There was nothing novel about the English arrangements after
1066. The Carolingian emperors of the ninth century had taken
the Jews in their lands under their wing, for example, and later
kings of France did something similar. There was also nothing
new about the price exacted by the kings for the protection they
provided. According to the twelfth-century legal tract known
as *The Laws of Edward the Confessor*, 'the Jews themselves and all
their possessions are the king's'.[24] It is not clear when, if ever, this
relationship was first formally clarified. However, this may have

happened during the reign of Henry I (1100–35). In 1201, King John (1199–1216) issued a royal charter which granted England's Jews the right 'freely and honourably to reside in our land and hold of us all things that they held of King Henry [I] our father's grandfather'.[25] Central to the experience of England's medieval Jewry, therefore, was the attitude of the post-Conquest kings towards it. All of the kings sought to control England's Jews and in the process to profit financially from their relationship with them. But, as will be seen, the methods they employed varied, and some kings appear to have taken their responsibilities as protectors more seriously than others. During the reigns of William I and his sons, however, there are few signs of the tension that was to dominate royal-Jewish relations for much of the next two centuries. Records are far from plentiful, but England, for example, does not seem to have been afflicted by the popular anti-Jewish sentiment and violence which accompanied the opening phases of the First Crusade in Germany's Rhineland.[26] Certainly no contemporary chronicler or historian, for whom such stories would have had a grisly attraction, mentioned anything happening in England comparable to the pogroms which took place there. Indeed, by 1100, England's Jewish community was probably still a fledgling one of which the bulk of the population remained largely unaware.

By 1135, by contrast, the English Jewry was well established and prosperous. However, there was still, as far as can be judged, only one settlement of any size, in London, although it is impossible to say how large it was in numerical terms. Of course, it is possible that Jews may have started to settle in places outside London before 1135.[27] However, the evidence for this is not conclusive, and the more obvious importance of London is in itself probably a reflection of the tightness of the control exercised over the movements of the Jews by the king and his officials. That is to say, the closer the Jews were kept to one of the main centres of royal government and to the Tower of

London, the more easily they could be protected, controlled and
supervised. This does not mean that London's Jews did not travel
across England to fairs and markets, but if they were permitted
to settle outside London, their activities and therefore their
money might fall into other than royal hands. Indeed, this is
what may have begun to happen after the death of Henry I. His
successor was his nephew Stephen (1135–54), but Stephen had
a rival for the throne, Henry I's daughter and nominated heir,
Matilda. As a result, from 1138 until 1153, England was in a state
of civil war or, as some historians have chosen to call it, 'anar-
chy'. In the absence of a masterful and dominant king during
the 1140s, many of Stephen's subjects began to make their own
arrangements in order to protect and secure their lands and
their livelihoods. Some great magnates entered into treaties of
mutual peace and friendship with each other, for example. Some
even minted their own coins, whilst lowlier men sought out
the patronage of lords in whom they could have confidence.
And it may be no coincidence that, as the grip of centralised
royal authority steadily loosened during Stephen's reign, Jewish
settlements began to spread across England.[28] There were Jewish
communities at Oxford by 1141, at Norwich by 1144 and at
Winchester by 1148, although it is not possible to say how firmly
established they were; and there is evidence of another community at Cambridge during the 1140s when Nigel, Bishop of
Ely pawned a jewelled cross and a gospel book to Jews there.[29] In
the absence of a strong royal protector, too, England's Jews may
have felt compelled to make new arrangements for their security, and thus it is no surprise to find local lords controlling and
supervising their own Jewries during this period. The Lincoln
Jewry may have flourished under the control of Earl Ranulf
of Chester, for example, who controlled that city for most of
the 1140s. And it has been suggested that the abbot of Bury St
Edmunds controlled a small Jewry there, although this may not
have been established until after Stephen's death.[30] Other such

'seigneurial Jewries' were certainly established in East Anglia by the start of Henry II's reign. Earl William II d'Albini founded a Jewry within the planned town he constructed around the great stone keep he built at Castle Rising in Norfolk. And others were created in the same county at Thetford and Bungay. In these two cases, the baron to whom the Jews would have looked for protection was Hugh Bigod, Earl of Norfolk. For the earl, this would have been just one more way of extending his political and economic control across Norfolk and Suffolk. However, it was also a reflection of his political allegiance. Earl Hugh had supported Stephen at the start of his reign, but had defected to Matilda's side in the civil war by the early 1140s. The principal Jewry in East Anglia then was probably at Norwich, a town loyal to Stephen. The earl's establishment of rival Jewries on his own lands was thus part of the wider political and military situation.[31]

Along with this increase in the number of Jewish settlements went the extension of credit and trading facilities and a growth in anti-Jewish sentiment. Such prejudices were not peculiarly English, of course, and it is fair to say that the 1140s witnessed a significant intensification of Jewish persecution on the continent. The preliminary stages of the Second Crusade, which was launched by Pope Eugenius III at the end of 1145, saw attacks on Jewish communities in the Rhineland despite the attempts of the Church's hierarchy, and of no less a figure than Bernard of Clairvaux himself, to prevent them; and there is evidence to suggest that King Stephen had to intervene in England to prevent Jews being attacked there at around the same time.[32] As has been seen, there had been attacks on the Jewish communities along the Rhine in 1096, after the First Crusade had been launched, but little if any of this active aggression seems to have been found in England at that time. However, that the 1140s witnessed increased antagonism towards the Jews in England at the same time as the Second Crusade was getting under way suggests the

extent to which England's Jews had become more prominent
members of society and more obvious targets for violence. And
it is in this context that the most notorious episode of the 1140s
concerning English Jews, the murder of William of Norwich in
1144, should be considered. According to a report contained in
the *Anglo-Saxon Chronicle*, which was written at Peterborough
in about 1155, in Stephen's reign:

> ...the Jews of Norwich bought a Christian child before Easter and
> tortured him with all the torture that our Lord was tortured with; and
> on Good Friday hanged him on a cross on account of our Lord and then
> buried him. They expected it would be concealed, but our Lord made
> it plain that he was a holy martyr, and the monks took him and buried
> him with ceremony in the monastery, and through our Lord he works
> wonderful and varied miracles, and he is called St. William.[33]

The truth behind this story is now impossible to recover, especially since the compiler of the *Chronicle* was basing his account
on the story of 'Little St William' as it had been written by the
Norwich monk Thomas of Monmouth between about 1149
and 1155.[34] All that can be said with a reasonable degree of
certainty is that, on Easter Saturday 1144, the dead body of a
twelve-year-old apprentice skinner called William was found
in woods near Norwich and immediately buried. Three weeks
later, William's uncle publicly charged the Jewish community in
Norwich with responsibility for William's murder; they had tortured and killed him and then dumped his body, it was alleged.
More than this, however, it was soon being claimed that this had
been a ritual killing and the product of a much wider Jewish
conspiracy: one such human sacrifice took place every Easter
somewhere in Europe, it was claimed, and these outrages were
designed to commemorate and celebrate the Jews' role in the
death of Christ. In April 1144, William's body was disinterred and
reburied in the monks' cemetery in Norwich. However, until

Thomas of Monmouth arrived there in about 1150 to become a monk in the cathedral priory, the story of William's death had attracted little wider attention, and its eventual notoriety was a consequence of Thomas's obsession with the development of William's cult. It was Thomas who first reported that William had been crucified, for example, and the story of William the Martyr as told by Thomas is probably the first known enunciation of the myth of Jewish ritual murder, the 'blood libel'.[35] Thus, 'he created a myth that affected Western mentality from the twelfth to the twentieth century and caused, directly or indirectly, far more deaths than William's murderer could ever have dreamt of committing'. Or put slightly differently, in Colin Richmond's words, 'A single Englishman was the sole begetter of a lie which had more life in it than most truths have; that lie led to terrible and untold suffering'.[36]

As for the king, his role and that of his officials in this episode is tantalisingly hinted at by some of the surviving accounts. According to Thomas of Monmouth, the Jews who had killed William, fearing they had been discovered as the culprits by a local worthy, fled to the sheriff, John of Chesney, the king's principal officer in the localities, a man 'who had been wont to be their refuge and their one and only protector'. Admittedly, they had to give him 100 marks in order to secure his protection on this occasion; but in accepting what could be interpreted as a bribe, John was only acting in the spirit of the relationship established between the English Jews and their royal lords. Later, Thomas described the circumstances in which the story of William's murder came to be repeated before the king himself. This time, the Jews of Norwich had initially complained to Stephen about the murder of a leading member of their community, Eleazar. According to the Jewish accusers, a local knight, Simon de Novers, who just happened to be in debt to Eleazar, had arranged the murder. Simon, however, defended by William Turbe, Bishop of Norwich, denied the charge when the case was

brought before the king. Eleazar had been killed by bandits on the
road, the bishop argued. Moreover, he went on, good Christian
folk should not have to face accusations of this kind from the very
people who had been responsible for the death of William the
Martyr in 1144. Indeed, the bishop claimed that Eleazar himself
did 'in conjunction with the other Jews then in the city, in his
house, as report says, miserably torment, kill and hide in a wood
a Christian boy'. And the murderers had escaped punishment
for this crime 'because Sheriff John opposed us and maintained
them'. When urged to act on this matter, the king's initial response
was to postpone the proceedings until the next general council
of clergy and barons. However, just before that council met in
London, 'the more sagacious of the Jews' obtained an audience
with the king 'by bribing his councillors, as report says, gave him,
it is said, a large sum of money, and succeeded with difficulty in
extorting a promise of favour'. They also tried to bribe Bishop
William, but he remained incorruptible and steadfast. Then, when
the king was finally reminded of the case during the London
council, he agreed only to postpone it 'to another season'.

Much of this story needs to be treated with caution. Thomas
of Monmouth's purpose in including it in his account of the
life and miracles of Little St William was polemical and it helped
him to illustrate the behaviour and characteristics of 'that most
crafty and avaricious race, the Jews'. They would never have
offered the king, the bishop or the sheriff money unless they
had been guilty, Thomas argued. Of course, the offers of money
may have been an indicator of guilt; it is impossible to know
for certain. It seems much more likely, however, that the Jews
wanted help and that the payments were intended to remind the
king and his sheriff of their responsibilities towards the Jews.[37]
As one medieval historian has recently and effectively put it,
'the king was the fount of justice but his waters did not run
freely'.[38] And something of the same dynamic also seems to have
been behind Stephen's treatment of the Jews of Oxford in the

1140s. In 1141, whilst Matilda controlled the city, she taxed the Jews there. When he recaptured it, Stephen demanded from the Oxford Jews a payment three and a half times greater than the one they had given his rival. When they refused, he threatened to burn down their houses in the city and only after one of the bigger houses had already been destroyed by fire did they agree to his demands. It is right, therefore, to describe the attitude of the post–Conquest English kings towards the Jews as 'acquisitive rather than benevolent'.[39]

Thus, between 1135 and 1154, the state of English Jewry was significantly changed. When King Stephen died, London was still by far the most important Jewish settlement, but new communities had been established across much of southern, central and eastern England. As a result, Jewish financial expertise had become readily available for a much larger number of Englishmen than ever before; Jewish credit, too, for it was probably during this period that moneylending became the primary focus of Jewish commercial activity. They would have carried on other business at the same time, and continued to exchange money and deal in plate, bullion and other luxury goods. However, it is likely that a decisive shift towards lending had been made by the time Henry II became king in 1154. They were providing a service which people wanted, and in doing so they would have been encouraged to spread their activities even further afield. There were problems to guard against, however. As the amount of Jewish wealth increased through lending, and as Jewish involvement in the lives of needy Christians deepened, the more resentment towards individual Jews and their communities was likely to grow. The second half of the twelfth century was to see England's Jewish communities thrive; but it was also the period during which hostility towards them began to be expressed in England more clearly and more violently than ever before.

2

The Jews in Angevin England 1154–1216

According to the chronicler William FitzStephen, who wrote during the reign of King Henry II (1154–89), after the chaos of Stephen's reign 'peace was everywhere and there emerged in safety from the towns and castles both merchants seeking fairs and Jews seeing creditors'.[1] And it is certainly fair to say that, under Henry II, England's Jews prospered. However, as the number of their settlements increased along with their wealth and influence, so did resentment towards them. Thus, by the time Richard I became king in 1189, the ground had been prepared for a furious anti-Jewish backlash. Richard and then his brother John (1199–1216) managed partially to rebuild the barricade which sheltered the Jews from violent persecution. But John in particular, in his remorseless quest for ready cash, was also responsible for the start of those processes whereby royal protection gradually developed into royal oppression.

In 1153, at Winchester, King Stephen and Henry of Anjou negotiated an end to the civil war which had afflicted England since the late 1130s. Stephen was to remain king during his lifetime, but he recognised Henry as his heir. Consequently, when Stephen died in 1154, Henry of Anjou became King Henry II in the most untroubled accession to the English throne for over a century. Henry II was the most powerful ruler in western Europe in the second half of the twelfth century. By the time he became king of England, he had already inherited his family lands, the county of Anjou; and he had also been given the duchy of Normandy by his father, Geoffrey, who had taken it from Stephen by conquest in the 1140s. And through his marriage to Eleanor of Aquitaine in 1152, Henry was also duke of Aquitaine, the great province which covered most of southern France. Along with England, therefore, Henry ruled a collection of lands (usually referred to by historians as The 'Angevin Empire') which stretched from the northern borders of England to the southern borders of France.

As for England's Jews, their 'empire' was expanding by the 1150s, too. This has been touched on in the previous chapter, but it is worth dwelling on here in a little more depth. In 1159, Henry II levied a tax or *donum* from England's Jews, and the receipts from this exercise are recorded on the pipe roll for 1158–9. Money was paid into the royal treasury by Jewish communities in no less than eleven different places. London clearly still retained its pre-eminent position amongst these communities, and paid well over a third (£133 6s 8d) of the total amount (£362 6s 8d) raised by the tax. Norwich came next in terms of the size of the amount paid (£44 6s 8d), followed by Lincoln (£40), Winchester and Cambridge (each paid £33 6s 8d) and Thetford (£30). Northampton and Bungay paid £15 each, whilst Oxford paid £13 6s 8d. Two other places are also mentioned in the records. £3 6s 8d came into the royal coffers from Gloucester and £1 6s 8d from Worcester.[2] Several things about this list are worth noting. The sums paid were in themselves not enormous, especially for a prosperous community like London. Nevertheless, they probably do represent settled Jewish populations of a reasonable size; although the small sums paid by Gloucester and Worcester may have come from a very small number of people, perhaps even a single Jew in the latter case. More important are the number of places which contributed to the tax and their geographical diversity. As yet, there appears to have been no Jewish presence in northern England (indeed, most of the communities mentioned in the 1159 list are in the south-east). However, a considerable change had taken place in the character of English Jewry, since only the London community had been mentioned in the pipe roll of 1129–30. What is more, most of these places were ports, albeit small ones, most had their own mints and most were near major fairs. The Jews settled in such places in order to change and lend money for those who needed it to trade. The presence of Bungay and Thetord on this royal list is also interesting for another reason. These were two of the 'seigneurial Jewries' referred to in the last chapter. By 1159, however, they appear to have been under royal supervision. Two years earlier, as part of his efforts to reassert royal authority in England after the civil war, Henry II had confiscated two of the castles, at Framlingham and Bungay, which were held by Hugh Bigod, Earl of Norfolk, the man who had probably established the Jewries at Thetford and Bungay. It is not unreasonable to assume that along with this went the stipulation that the Jews under Hugh's control should remain so no longer. The other seigneurial Jewry mentioned earlier was at Bury St Edmunds. Nothing appears concerning this community on the 1159 list (it may not have been established yet). However, in 1158, the sheriff of Suffolk had paid £13 6s 8d into the treasury *pro Judeis*. It has been suggested that this represents an early *donum* payment. If so, perhaps Henry II had reasserted his authority over the abbot's Jewry, too.[3]

Henry II was certainly a strong, masterful king and the kind of protector England's Jews would probably have been happy to have. His favourable treatment of Jews was notorious, and he may have issued a charter confirming and clarifying their status in England.[4] Unfortunately, if he did so, it has not survived, although charters later issued by his sons, Richard and John, appear to mention it. It is possible to piece together the main points of it from them. Amongst the most important terms of John's charter of April 1201, the right of the Jews of England and Normandy to reside in their kingdom or duchy was confirmed, as was their right to hold property and to retain all the liberties and customs which they had enjoyed under Henry I. Significantly, too, John's charter stated that Jews might go 'wherever they wish with all their possessions, *as our property*' [my italics]. Jewish heirs were permitted to succeed to their fathers' money and debts; they could trade in all things 'except those which belong to the Church and bloodstained cloth'. Property held as security could be legally sold a year and a day after an unpaid debt became due, and various provisions dealt with the settlement of disputes among Jews and between Jews and Christians.[5] Of course, the Angevin kings' concern for English Jewry was by no means purely selfless. According to one contemporary, England's Jews at this time were 'happy and respected' under royal protection. However, Henry II was also said to be guilty of favouring the Jews 'more than was right... because of the great advantage which he saw was to be had from their usuries'.[6]

It is certainly true that Henry II used the Jews as a source of funds. For the first dozen or so years of his reign, however, he does not appear to have borrowed significantly from them, and his principal providers of credit were Christians.[7] Until his death in 1166, the king's main lender was William Cade of St Omer in Flanders. Cade was an immensely wealthy man, and his fortune probably derived originally from the wool trade which linked the Flemish and English economies. The king was by no means his only debtor: 'he would accommodate anybody and he had terms to suit every sort and condition of men'.[8] However, it is likely that the king borrowed more extensively than most. It is impossible to know exactly how much Cade lent to the king; the only surviving evidence concerning their relationship is in the form of records on the pipe rolls of repayments made to Cade by the king or his officials. These amount to some £5,600 between 1156 and 1166, and, not least because their relationship was almost certainly established before 1154, this figure probably represents only a part of the total amount that the king received from Cade. For one thing, from the beginning of the reign until 1161, Cade was granted the revenues of the town of Dover by the king, almost certainly as a form of ongoing repayment. Other Christian financiers lent to the king, too. William Trentegerons of Rouen, and his wife, Emma, who was directly involved in the family business, probably lent to Henry before 1154, but once again the only evidence of their activities comes from the pipe rolls which, between 1156 and 1163, record payments of just under £2,000 being made to them from royal funds. Again, this is probably only a part of what they actually lent. Like Cade, Trentegerons was granted the revenues of an important town, in his case Southampton, from 1156 to 1163. And the revenues of Northampton were awarded to another Christian lender, Robert FitzSavin, to whom repayments are recorded on the pipe rolls between 1155 and 1171. A fourth, Ralph Waspail, is more obscure; occasional payments, including one of £600 in 1161–2, are recorded on the pipe rolls between 1157 and 1173.

There was Jewish lending to the crown during these years, too, but it seems to have been on a much less extensive scale than that by Christians. Between 1157 and 1164 the pipe rolls record repayments of over £500 made by the king to Isaac, the son of Rabbi Josce who had been at the head of London's Jewish community in 1130. However, the royal policy was soon to change. For reasons which are unclear, Henry II effectively stopped using the services of Christian lenders after 1163–4. Some small repayments to William Cade, totalling only £116, are recorded on the pipe rolls for 1165–6. No repayments to William Trentegerons are recorded at all after 1161–2, and Ralph Waspail disappears from the records after 1163. Only Robert FitzSavin continued to have any contact with the king. Perhaps the death of William Cade in 1166 led the king to rethink his approach to credit; its aftermath might also have led Christian financiers to rethink the wisdom of getting involved with Henry II. On Cade's death, the king seized all of his bonds, which had a face value of about £5,000, and set about collecting the sums due himself. It was his right to do this, he claimed, as on the death of usurers their estates came to him. And there is a degree of contemporary support for this position. That great guide to the history and procedure of the royal Exchequer, *The Dialogue of the Exchequer*, made it clear that, when a usurer died, 'all he had falls to the King'; and the legal treatise known as *Glanvill* held that 'all the chattels of a usurer... go to the lord king'.[9] Such views would certainly have suited Henry II in 1166, but both works were written several years after that date and they may even have had Cade's case in mind when dealing with the issue. Perhaps the king's seizure of Cade's bonds had made the law rather than followed it. And regardless of their legal merits, Henry's actions may have acted to deter Christian lenders dealing with him. There is little sign, for example, that William Cade's son, Ernulf, who had worked closely with his father before 1166, attempted to rebuild his father's English business after the latter's death.

Perhaps the hardening attitude of the Church towards usury also played a part in the king's change of direction. Usury, the lending and borrowing of money at interest, was a sin according

to Leviticus 25:25-38 and Deuteronomy 23:19-21, and Luke
(6:35) quoted Christ as saying 'Lend without expecting any
return'. By the second half of the twelfth century, the ecclesiastical authorities were keener than ever to deter Christians from
practising usury. In 1163, for example, the Council of Tours had
condemned 'open' usury, where the payment of interest was
obvious. And in 1179, the Third Lateran Council condemned
usury again and ordered usurers to be excluded from the
community. Despite such measures, however, Christian mon-
eylenders such as William FitzIsabel and Gervase and Henry of
Cornhill certainly continued to operate in England at around
this time. It is more likely, however, that Henry II stopped using
Christian lenders in the mid-1160s and turned to Jewish ones
instead because they were rich and easier to exploit. Between
1165 and 1167, repayments to Isaac totalling some £1,575 are
recorded on the pipe rolls. At the same time, a new lender
had made his services available to the king. During these years,
repayments amounting to £420 were made to Aaron of Lincoln.
Aaron was to become the most important Jewish financier of
the twelfth century, and perhaps the richest man in England. He
made his fortune in a variety of ways; by buying up the debts
of other Jews, by pawnbroking and by securing rent-charges.
However, his chief business was moneylending. Born probably
before 1130, Aaron was well established in Lincoln by the mid-
1160s, and over the next twenty years his credit network came to
reach into almost every English county. When he died in 1186,
Aaron's property was confiscated by the king, and a special office,
'the Exchequer of Aaron', was set up by the royal administration
to administer the collection of his debts. It was found that Aaron
was owed no less than £18,466 by more than 400 debtors.
However, the total value of his estate on his death is unknown,
and it may have approached £100,000. A list was drawn up of
all Aaron's bonds, and the fragment of this which survives from
the county of Rutland gives some idea of the way in which the

credit market operated in the second half of the twelfth century. The eleven Rutland debts range from £115 owed by Aubrey de Dammartin to 6s 8d owed by someone called Truve. Within this range, other debts were owed by individual churchmen, one religious house, Brooke Priory, and a royal chamberlain, William Mauduit. Most of the debts were short-term, and the principal sums were repayable after a year. Interest was payable either from the time the loan was contracted, or after the time at which full repayment was due, as a sort of penalty clause. Interest rates were set at either 22 per cent, 44 per cent or 66 per cent (in other words at one, two or three pence per pound per week). The debts were secured by pledges of land or by reputable third parties who were prepared to act as guarantors for a particular debtor. Most of Aaron's loans, it seems, were of small amounts made to relatively humble individuals. Most of his money, however, was lent as large sums to high-status men (knights and barons) and to religious houses; ten Cistercian abbeys owed Aaron more than £4,250 between them in 1186. It is certainly fair to say that 'the net of indebtedness was wide and deep'. It was all too easy to become entangled in it.[10]

By the late 1160s Aaron had assumed the role of principal royal creditor. The last recorded repayments to Isaac, made in 1168, were trivial, amounting to only £21. Thereafter, he disappears from the records. In 1169–70, by contrast, repayments of over £533 were made to Aaron. He was not the only Jewish lender, however. Benedict, son of Sarah and Eliab (or Jurnet) of Norwich, the latter one of the wealthiest Jews in England at the time and the dominant figure in Norwich's Jewish community, both appear in the records from the late 1160s. However, whilst this shift from royal reliance on Christian lending to a similar reliance on Jewish lending was certainly significant, its importance should not be overstated. The sums raised were sizeable, but they probably formed only a relatively small part of total royal revenue. There are several years during the early

1170s, for example, when no loan repayments are recorded on
the pipe rolls at all, although debts could have been repaid in
other, less formal, ways; through the royal wardrobe, for example,
for which no records exist. In any event, Henry II only relied
on individual Jewish lenders until around 1175–6. Perhaps in
an effort to deal with increasing royal demands, between 1176
and 1179, loans were made to the king by a series of Jewish
syndicates or consortia. In 1175, Isaac reappears in the records
alongside Jurnet of Norwich. Together they paid Henry II four
gold marks in order to be allowed to form such a syndicate.
This initial effort appears to have failed, but in 1176 Isaac, his
brother Abraham and Aaron of Lincoln organised themselves
into a group. Together they were repaid £600 in that year. A
third partnership soon appeared as the previous one disappeared
from view. This time, its members were Jurnet of Norwich
and his brother Benedict, Moses le Brun of London, and Josce
Quatrebuches. For mysterious reasons, this group also failed,
and its members were obliged to pay £4,000 to obtain the
king's pardon in 1177. Jurnet had paid his one-third share of
this (£1,333 6s 8d) by 1181. The last consortium of this kind
was established between 1177 and 1179 by Benedict, son of
Sarah, Josce (probably the son of Isaac), Dieudonné l'Eveske
and Vives. These were all members of the London community,
and, on the face of things, they were the most successful of all
such groups. Between 1177 and 1179, they were repaid £1,890
by the king.[11]

Despite the apparent success of the London syndicate, this
phase of the relationship between the king and the English
Jewry appears to have come to an end by 1180. Thereafter, the
king's approach changed again. Loans from individuals were no
longer taken out and the consortia ceased operating. Henry's
main financial interest in the Jews now lay in taxing them as
a community. It is possible that he had been attracted to such
an option by the workings of the consortia themselves. In 1177,

when the third partnership failed and was forced to pay its way out of trouble, half of the £4,000 penalty was charged to Moses le Brun, and the whole English Jewry was made responsible for paying £666 of this. It has also been suggested that, given their 'relative insignificance', the members of the fourth partnership did not themselves lend money to the king; rather, 'the inference is that they were no more than agents, intermediaries between the king and the English Jewry'.[12] If this was the case, it is not surprising that Henry II quickly came to see the potential size of the sums to be squeezed out of England's Jewish community as a whole. There was nothing new about this. The *donum* of 1159 has already been mentioned, and it was almost certainly not the only one of its kind before 1180. However, it is impossible to be sure how frequently such taxes or 'tallages' were imposed. The first for which hard evidence survives after 1159 is the tallage which was ordered by Henry II at the court he held at Guildford at Christmas 1186. One chronicler, Gervase of Canterbury, claimed that it raised no less than £60,000.[13] Now there is no way of verifying this, as the records which survive concern only the arrears of the tallage collected during Richard I's reign. It is impossible to know what proportion of the total collected these arrears represent. Nevertheless, the 1186 tallage was obviously large and burdensome. The weightiest burden fell on some of those financiers already mentioned: Le Brun's assessment was £6,666 and Jurnet's £6,000, although the latter was eventually reduced to £1,221. Regardless of this, another tallage, this time limited expressly to £6,666, was imposed on the English Jewry before Henry II's death.[14] Both of these impositions may have had something to do with Henry's crusading plans; the so-called 'Saladin Tithe' for the relief of the Holy Land was imposed in 1188. Whatever the reasons behind the Jewish tallages of Henry's last years, however, a new chapter had opened in the story of the relationship between the king and his Jews. By 1189, 'the Crown's financial demands rose to a crescendo', and 'instead of having their ability utilised, as hitherto, [the Jews] could henceforth be exploited, by a facile method which was to end in their ruin'.[15]

But English Jewry was nearly ruined by violence rather than financial oppression in the years immediately following the death of Henry II and the accession of Richard I in 1189. Following the murder of Little St William at Norwich in 1144, hostility towards England's Jews had become steadily more vocal and violent. Further accusations of ritual murder were made against the Jewish communities at Gloucester in 1168, after which a shrine dedicated to 'St Harold' was erected in the abbey; at Bury St Edmunds in 1181, where the death of 'St. Robert' was remembered; and at Bristol in 1183, where a Christian boy named Adam was alleged to have been killed by Samuel of Bristol who, after also killing his own wife, repented and converted to Christianity.[16] Developments abroad provide a wider context for these events. For example, in 1179 the Third Lateran Council had urged Christians to minimise their contact with Jews. And in France in 1180, the new French king, Philip II 'Augustus', who claimed similar rights to the English king over the Jews in his kingdom, issued an edict which led to the arrest of many Jews. Then, in 1182, all Jews were formally expelled from the king's own lands, and they were not allowed to return until 1198.[17] Such episodes may also have stirred up more anti-Jewish feeling in England. Probably most significant of all, however, were events in the Holy Land. On 4 July 1187 the Muslim leader Saladin crushed the army of the Christian Kingdom of Jerusalem at the battle of Hattin. He then proceeded to overrun the lands which had been held by the Christian settlers for much of the twelfth century, and Jerusalem fell once again into the hands of the infidel. The shock caused by these events when news of them reached western Europe was enormous, and a fresh outburst of crusading enthusiasm soon followed. And, as they had at the start of the First and

Second Crusades, the Jews found themselves in the firing line. Their wealth provided a ready source of crusading funds, and, like Saladin and his hordes, they were the enemies of Christ. Indeed, by the end of the twelfth century, many of the later and lasting views of what it meant to be Jewish had begun to crystallise in the minds of the Christian majority. Hatred of the Jews was deepening, since 'as well as unpopular moneylender, a stereotypical view prevailed of the Jew as a sorcerer, murderer, necromancer, cannibal, poisoner, blasphemer, international conspirator and Devil's disciple'.[18]

In England, matters began to get out of hand following the coronation of Richard I at Westminster in September 1189. Leading Jews from all over England came to London for the event, hoping to obtain the new king's favour and protection. According to William of Newburgh, who provides the fullest account of these events,

> those enemies of truth were on the watch, lest, perchance, the prosperity which they had enjoyed under the preceding monarch should smile upon them less favourably under the new king. They wished that his first acts should be honoured by them in the most becoming manner, thinking that undiminished favour would be secured by ample gifts.

Richard, however, refused to allow the Jewish delegation into Westminster Abbey or into the hall where he feasted after his consecration; for fear of their magic, the credulous Matthew Paris later alleged.[19] But unfortunately for them, some of the Jews were swept up within the exuberant crowd which had gathered outside the palace, and pushed inside. One Christian then remembered the terms of the royal order against them, and began to beat one of the Jews. At this, a full-scale attack on the Jews was launched by the hysterical crowd. In William of Newburgh's words again,

> ...a tumult arose. The lawless and furious mob, thinking that the king
> had commanded it and supported them, as they thought, by his royal
> authority, rushed like the rest upon the multitude of Jews who stood
> watching at the door of the palace. At first they beat them unmercifully
> with their fists; but soon becoming more enraged, they took sticks and
> stones. The Jews then fled away; and, in their flight, many were beaten,
> so that they died, and others were trampled under foot and perished.

This was by no means the end of the episode. A mob, 'eager for plunder and for the blood of a people hateful to all men', soon gathered, having convinced itself that the king had authorised a wholesale extermination of London's Jews. And 'from three o'clock until sunset' they were besieged in their houses. These well-built residences were able to withstand the furious onslaught, but their roofs were more vulnerable and were set on fire. A number of Jews were burnt to death and others were killed on fleeing their burning homes. Further slaughter was only prevented when the angry crowd turned its attention to plundering the Jews' property; 'their avarice overcame their cruelty'. On learning of what was happening, the king sent his justiciar, Ranulf Glanville, to quell the disturbance; but he was unable to do anything to stop it and the plundering continued until the following morning.[20]

There is no way of knowing how many Jews were killed during the London riot of 3–4 September. In another account of it, Ephraim of Bonn claimed that thirty Jews were killed, including Jacob of Orleans, 'a famous rabbi'. Also according to Ephraim, others Jews committed suicide after killing their own children, in order to prevent them falling into the hands of the Christian mob.[21] Two Jews of York, Josce and Benedict, are the only individuals mentioned by name in William of Newburgh's account. They attempted to flee when the violence began, but Benedict was captured, taken to a church and forcibly baptised. The next day, he recanted of his conversion before the king and died of his injuries some days later at Northampton. During their audience, King Richard had asked Benedict whether he was a Christian. 'He replied that he had been baptised by the Christians by force but that he had always been a Jew in spirit and wished to die as one'. The king then turned to the archbishop of Canterbury for guidance: 'If he will not serve God, let him serve the devil', came Baldwin's contemptuous reply.[22]

The king was furious about what had happened. The Jews were under his protection, and so the attacks were an assault on his dignity and power as well as his purse. Nevertheless, for various reasons, there was little that the government could do. Too many people had been involved in the violence for any sort of general punishment to be effective or prudent; in William of Newburgh's words, 'it would be utterly impossible to enforce the rigour of royal censure upon such an indefinite multitude of guilty persons'. What is more, the king was eager to leave England and begin his crusade. Three people were hanged, but for offences committed towards Christians during the riot, and royal letters were dispatched ordering that Jews across England should be left in peace. Beyond this, however, little action was taken. Until Richard finally sailed from England in December 1189, there were no more episodes of this kind; but once he had left the kingdom, it was not long before the violence resumed. Beginning in East Anglia in February 1190, there were anti-Jewish attacks at Lynn (a Jewish community had moved there from Castle Rising in Henry II's reign), where much of the town was destroyed by the fires which accompanied the riots, and Norwich; and then at Stamford, Lincoln, Colchester, Thetford and Ospringe in Kent.[23] At Bury St Edmunds on Palm Sunday 1190, fifty-seven Jews were massacred. The survivors were then expelled from the town at the request of the abbot.[24] The most notorious episode of all, however, took place at York.

The York Jewry was a relatively recent creation.[25] The city was not mentioned in the list of contributors to the *donum* of 1159, and it is probable that no settled Jewish community was established there before the 1170s. By 1190, it probably numbered about 150, and its leaders were the financiers Josce and Benedict, the same two men who appeared at Westminster for the coronation of Richard I. Josce and Benedict were substantial lenders, and the lists of their debtors were lengthy. More importantly, many of those debtors were influential men of means, northern barons and knights who, in order to raise money on credit, were compelled to pledge their lands to their Jewish lenders as security. Josce, Benedict, their families and their associates were bound to be objects of suspicion and foci for hostility. Their obvious wealth did not help, either: Josce's house in York resembled 'a noble citadel in the scale and stoutness of its construction', according to William of Newburgh.[26] Benedict's house was probably no less impressive, and it was his dwelling that bore the brunt of the first attack at the beginning of March 1190. Benedict by now was dead, and the occupants of the house were at the mercy of a band of armed raiders. They were a mixed group: William of Newburgh described how the nobility and more respectable citizens of York refused to join in the rioting, but no scruples deterred those about to depart on crusade or the labourers and the young men of the city, as well as 'a very great mob of country people, and not a few military men… as if each one sought his own private advantage, and something great for himself'.[27] All of those trapped in Benedict's house, including his widow and children, were killed. Consequently, the next day, York's surviving Jews, led by Josce, made their way to the royal castle ('Clifford's Tower') and asked for shelter and protection. All but a few of them were inside the castle when Josce's own house was attacked a few days later. At this point, the relationship between the Jews in the castle and the castellan began to break down. The castellan was Richard Malebisse, known to his creditors as 'the Evil Beast'. He was heavily in debt to Jewish lenders, and had no reason to protect his new guests with any enthusiasm. The Jews therefore locked the castellan out of the keep, and he in turn requested help from the sheriff of Yorkshire, John Marshall. Marshall fatefully decided to besiege the castle. By the time he had reconsidered this decision it was too late, and the crowd, stirred into frenzy by a maverick white-robed hermit, was out of his control. The Jews withstood the siege until 16 March, but on the evening of that day, siege machines were moved into place, and it became only a matter of time before the castle was captured. A decision now had to be taken by the Jews within its walls, and the discussion was led by Rabbi Jomtob of Joigny, an eminent scholar, who had perhaps come to York in the aftermath of the expulsion from France eight years earlier. The rabbi urged his comrades to follow Hebraic tradition and kill themselves before others did it for them. Josce proceeded to cut the throats of his wife and his sons, and other fathers then did the same to their families. They in their turn were probably killed by Rabbi Jomtob, who ended the killing by cutting Josce's throat and then his own. Not all of the York Jews died in this way, however. Some of them had decided to convert to Christianity rather than die, and Malebisse promised them mercy if they came out of the castle. But on leaving their refuge on 17 March, they were massacred as they attempted to surrender. The leading conspirators, 'combining barbarity with business', then went straight to York Minster where they seized the copies of Jewish loans deposited there for safe-keeping.[28] These bonds were then burned in the middle of the church.

Having been displeased at the attacks on Jews in London in 1189, and having expressly ordered that England's Jews be left in peace, King Richard was bound to be outraged at what had happened in York. It fell to his chancellor, William Longchamp, Bishop of Ely, to return to England and to seek out and punish the culprits. Early in May 1190, he travelled to York with an armed force under the command of his brother, Henry. The citizens of York, protesting their collective innocence, managed to pay themselves out of trouble. As in London, it would have been difficult to punish them all; but Longchamp also took hostages from them and sent them into custody at Northampton. As for the leaders of the attacks (several of whom had fled to Scotland in their immediate aftermath), they were more harshly treated. John Marshall was relieved of his position as sheriff of Yorkshire and replaced by another of Longchamp's brothers, Osbert. The lands of Richard Malebisse and his kinsman, William Percy, were confiscated, along with the lands of several others. The York massacre probably also dealt a blow to the royal finances, and, in its wake, the government established new mechanisms and procedures which were designed to protect and exploit the Jews more efficiently. There was already something to build on here in the shape of the office set up after 1186 to administer the debts of Aaron of Lincoln. So, after the massacres of the early 1190s, the responsibilities of those officials in charge of this department, 'the justices of the Jews', were expanded so that soon they were made responsible for the tallages imposed on the English Jewry by the king, loans owed to Jews, as well as the debts owed to them by Christians which had fallen into the king's own hands. In the thirteenth century, this institution was formally known as the Exchequer of the Jews, and records of its business and routines survive from 1218. Its role was more than purely financial. Based on the west side of Westminster Hall, and 'covering all aspects of the relations of the Jewry to the Crown', it also came to act as a court which could deal with disputes involving Jews. Only Christians acted as judges in this court; but alongside them would have sat the *presbyter Judeorum* or archpresbyter. He was usually one of the wealthier members of the Jewish community, but he was not put in office by his own people. He was appointed by the king as an authority on Jewish affairs, custom and tradition and, during the thirteenth century, the archpresbyter was the administrative head of the English Jewish community.[29]

By then, other procedures and methods concerning English Jewry had been developed and refined. This process appears to have begun systematically in 1194. First of all in that year, the teams of judges who embarked on their 'eyre', or nation-wide tour of the kingdom in order to administer justice in the king's name, were explicitly ordered to inquire into the events of 1190. Anyone suspected of involvement in the attacks who had not yet made his peace was to be arrested. Furthermore, the affairs of the victims prior to their death were to be inves-tigated: what they had held, what they had been owed. All of this was to be taken into royal custody in an attempt to recoup some of the financial losses the king had suffered. An attempt was also made to systematise and standardise the process of Jewish lending across the country. The lending system itself was to be overseen by two officials of the Exchequer, William of Saint-Mère-Église, a future bishop of London, and William de Chimillé, whilst henceforth loans were only to be contracted and repaid at one of six or seven designated centres and before a panel of two Christians, two Jews and two clerks in each place. These places were not specified in 1194, but it is reason-able to assume that the government had London, Norwich, Lincoln and Winchester in mind, and probably two or three from Oxford, Bristol, Cambridge, Northampton, Nottingham and Gloucester. The loans were to be completed in duplicate, in the form of a 'chirograph', in the presence of these officials; one copy was to be kept by the lender and the other deposited in a chest or *archa* secured with three locks and seals. Finally, every Jewish lender was obliged to swear that he would have all his transactions registered in this way.[30] These new regula-tions enabled the king to collect the debts of deceased Jewish lenders with ease and certainty; moreover, in future, even if the Jews themselves were attacked, records of their loans would be preserved and there would be no repeat of what had happened after the destruction of the York bonds in 1190. Thus the York massacre had a long-term significance beyond the shock it sent through Europe's Jewish communities; and it is quite fair to say that it 'was not only a tragedy but an influential tragedy: it helped to promote the closest relationship between state and Jewry yet seen in western Europe and to bring about a decisive transformation in the constitutional position of the medieval English Jews'.[31]

The 1190s, therefore, were a decade of crucial importance in the history of England's medieval Jewry. It should not be forgotten, however, that all of the measures implemented by Richard I, whilst designed better to protect the Jews from physical attack, were primarily intended to make their financial exploitation more systematic and methodical. 'How typical it was', Colin Richmond has written, 'that the consequence of such a tragedy (on such a scale, in England's second city) was more and, therefore, worse government for the Jews'.[32] Richard, indeed, was as keen to profit from his relationship with the Jews as his father had been. He had a crusade to pay for, as well as a huge ransom following his capture and imprisonment in Germany on his return from the Holy Land. At the start of his reign he levied a Jewish tallage of £1,333, and after he returned to England from Germany another levy of £3,333 was ordered at a council held at Northampton at Easter 1194. In addition, at around the same time, it was agreed that the Jews should contribute £2,000 to the cost of Richard's ransom. In the space of no more than five years, therefore, £6,666 had been demanded by the king from his Jewish subjects.[33] Of course, it is impossible to know for sure just how much of this money was actually paid. The surviving receipts for the Northampton *donum* of 1194, for example, show payment of £1,742 9s 2d, about half the total sum assessed.[34] These records are interesting for more than just the payments they record, however. Twenty-one separate Jewish communities contributed to the tax. Taking into account the three which had been destroyed in 1190 (York, Stamford and

Lynn) and a fourth which had been dissolved (Bury), therefore, the number of provincial Jewries in England had more
than doubled since only eleven communities had contributed
to the *donum* of 1159. The London community provided over
a quarter of the total paid in 1194 (£471 6s 3d), whilst Lincoln
and Canterbury ranked next with payments of £277 16s 3d and
£242 14s 4d respectively. The Northampton and Gloucester
Jewries each contributed well over £100, whilst those from
Cambridge and Worcester approached this. But the surviving records also detail payments towards the tax by individual
Jews, not just the total contributions of each community. Thus
three-quarters of the London total was provided by only eight
men, whilst only five men paid over half of the Lincoln Jewry's
contribution. And smaller communities appear to have been
even more reliant on wealthy individuals. Between half and
three-quarters of the total payments of the Winchester, Oxford
and Colchester Jewries were made by single contributors, for
example. And the largest of all the individual contributions to
the tax, £115 6s 8d by Jacob of Canterbury, amounted to just
under half of his community's total. By 1194, the increase in
English Jewries which had taken place since the 1150s was certainly striking; but so was the concentration of wealth in the
hands of a relatively small number of powerful magnates.

Fortunately, the state of the evidence improves in John's reign,
and a fuller picture of the Jewry's financial relations with the king
can be painted. Initially after 1199, there was little to suggest that
John would be significantly more exacting than his predecessors. To be sure, the royal charter he issued in April 1201 which
confirmed the rights of the Jews of England and Normandy to
dwell in the country and to enjoy all the rights and privileges
granted by John's predecessors was only obtained at a cost of
£2,666 13s 4d, payable in four instalments.[35] However, most of
those who contributed to this payment would have accepted
it as a necessary price for continuing royal protection. In July

1203, for example, presumably because they were being attacked
or harassed in some way, John was forced to remind the mayor
of London that the Jews were under his protection and that
violence towards them was unacceptable: 'If we had given our
peace to a dog', John stated in a phrase expressive both of his
own and of a wider attitude to the Jews, 'it ought to be invio-
lably observed'.[36]

But there was a very fine line between graceless royal
protection of this kind and royal exploitation; and the Jewry's
vulnerability in the hands of a grasping and desperate king soon
became apparent. Between 1202 and 1204, King John struggled
unsuccessfully to hold on to his duchy of Normandy in the
face of a sustained military attack by King Philip II 'Augustus'
(1180–1223) of France. In the end, with Philip's capture of the
ducal capital, Rouen, in June 1204, Normandy was lost; and,
in the following two years, so was the bulk of the rest of King
John's continental lands. The collapse of the Angevin Empire
was an event of huge long-term importance, as the balance
of power in Europe was fundamentally shifted in the French
king's favour.[37] For England's Jews, though, its significance was
also great. The link between England and Normandy having
been severed after 1204, the English Jewry's scope for contact
with its parent community across the English Channel was limited; cross-Channel trade and the general conduct of business
would also have become more difficult. The most direct impact,
however, was on the English Jews' financial relationship with
their royal protector. John was determined to win back his lost
French lands, but he knew that in order to do this he would
need money on a scale hitherto never collected by an English
king. For the next ten years, John used every traditional financial
device, and many novel ones, in his attempt to build up a huge
war chest.[38] But it was from 1207 that the king really began to
increase the pressure, and the Jews were not spared his attention.
In that year he levied a tallage of £2,666 from them, and in the

same year he also demanded 10 per cent of the value of their bonds from Jewish lenders along with precise details of all the transactions in question.[39] But it was in 1210 that the hammer-blow fell. In that year the so-called 'Bristol tallage' was imposed, and although the precise size of it is unclear, it is said to have been in the region of £44,000.[40] However large it actually was, its enormous size was almost certainly unprecedented (it was 'yet another new departure in extortionate fiscality' on John's part, according to Stacey), and it may have been prompted by the king's angry suspicion that he had not been paid everything he considered himself entitled to from the Jews in 1207.[41] The imposition of the tallage itself was preceded in 1210, according to one chronicler, by the arrest and imprisonment of all Jews, male and female, across the whole of England.[42] Whether every Jew was taken or not, certainly those who mattered financially were. Then all of the lenders' records relating to their bonds and transactions were confiscated and enrolled, perhaps in an attempt to check the sufficiency of what had been paid three years before. The king must have become convinced that the Jews had been guilty of widespread evasion; or at least he probably used this as a good enough excuse to exploit them further. Some prominent members of the community were deliberately made examples of. The leader of the Jewish community in Norwich, Isaac, the son of Jurnet of Norwich, was forced to promise the king £6,666, to be paid off at the rate of one mark daily for the next thirty years; he still ended up in the Tower of London and his debt was still being paid in 1220. Isaac of Canterbury was hanged and his possessions sold. One Bristol Jew is said to have been held in captivity and to have had one of his teeth knocked out every day until he paid what he owed.[43] It is clear from its size that the tallage was designed to be as punitive as it was productive. Even the poorest members of the community were forced to pay forty shillings each or else leave the kingdom; many must have taken the latter option, leading to a substantial reduction in the size of the English Jewry. It is not clear again just how much of the tallage of 1210 was ever collected, but it must be right to say that 'the year 1210 marks a turning-point in the history of the English Jewry'; it was indeed 'a black year' for England's Jews.[44]

Pressure was put on the Jews from other directions during John's reign, too. For example, the king was determined to optimise the amounts of money he received by virtue of his position as every Jew's heir. It was settled law that every Jew was royal property. In the words of one thirteenth-century legal tract, 'Truly the Jew can have nothing which belongs to himself, because whatever he acquires he acquires not for himself but for the king'.[45] When a Jewish lender died, his debts came automatically into the king's hands. The king then had a choice. He might allow the son of the deceased lender to take over his father's business; albeit at a price, of course, usually a third of the value of the deceased's estate. Thus, in 1244 the heirs of the great financiers David of Oxford and Leo of York paid £3,333 and £4,666 respectively in order to succeed to their father's estates.[46] Or the king might decide to collect the debts himself, in which case they would be entered in the royal records as outstanding sums due to the king.[47] However, in the early 1200s, many of these so-called *debita Judeorum* had been outstanding since the reign of Henry II and Richard I, and few systematic steps had been taken to collect them by John's predecessors. Indeed, by the time John became king, many of the debts were owed by the sons and heirs of the original debtors. In 1207, however, this hitherto fairly easy-going royal attitude towards these debts was abandoned, and John ordered that all of those whose debts to Aaron of Lincoln, who had died in 1186, were still outstanding should pay up or lose their lands. This in itself did not affect the finances of the Jewish lenders directly. But it bore down upon Christian borrowers, whose hostility towards the Jews was only likely to be increased by the implementation of these new measures. Furthermore, in 1210, as has been seen, in order to enable the Jews to pay the huge tallage of that year, John ordered that the debts of all living Jews should be taken into his hands and collected. This was a radical extension in the scope of the previous system, where the king's personal interest in Jewish loans only arose after the lender had died. The Jews were now being seen as the agents of the king's hated financial policies, and the resentment of borrower towards lender was only bound to increase as John's unpopularity deepened. After all, *debita Judeorum* have been described as both 'a major source of income to the king and one of the main instruments of financial persecution of the aristocracy'.[48]

After John foiled a plot to assassinate him in 1212, one of the conciliatory gestures he made was to relax somewhat the operation of this system. However, the issue was still a live one by the time civil war broke out in 1215. In May of that year John's opponents occupied London, and on doing so they were quick to attack the London Jewry, burning and demolishing houses; the stone was used to repair the walls of the city.[49] And in Magna Carta itself, which brought a temporary halt to the conflict after it was sealed and issued in the middle of June 1215, there is some indication of the grievances created by royal manipulation of the system of Jewish lending. Chapter 10 of the Charter provided that debts due to Jews or other usurers should carry no interest during the minority of an underage heir; and also that, if the debts of such an heir fell into the king's hands, no interest should be charged then either. And chapter 11 required that widows and children of those indebted to the Jews should be provided for from the husband's estates before any debt was repaid; repayments were only to be taken from what was left of the estate after provision had been made.[50] It is not unreasonable to infer from these clauses that, in John's unscrupulous hands, the system had been subject to widespread abuse. However, it is also striking, given their political sensitivity and the way that

John had manipulated the system of Jewish debts, that Jewish
matters were not dealt with more extensively in the charter;
chapters 10 and 11 were 'superficial', it has been said. Perhaps,
in the negotiations leading up to its creation, the rebel barons
had been unable to extract more meaningful concessions from
John; one of the many compromises they were forced to make
at Runnymede in the search for an end to the civil war. Or
perhaps, as Holt has suggested, this was an area on to which
even John's opponents were reluctant to transgress. The king's
right to exploit his Jewish subjects as he saw fit was recognised
and acknowledged, and the two clauses 'reveal a healthy respect
for existing usages and rights'.[51]

By 1216, therefore, having spread widely through England,
and having significantly increased the sophistication and range of
their business operations, England's Jews were on the defensive.
Royal pressure on their finances increased from the 1170s, and in
the 1190s they had been subjected to vicious persecution across
the kingdom. Physically attacked and economically squeezed by
the start of the thirteenth century, they would have had little
time to recover before John's financial policies bore down on
them with a previously unknown ferocity. Moreover, with the
resumption of civil war after John's repudiation of Magna Carta,
England was in chaos and the political outlook was unclear. In
May 1216, Louis, the son of King Philip 'Augustus' of France,
had landed in Kent at the invitation of John's opponents, and
there was a real possibility that England might become a French
satellite. John's death in October 1216 might, in more stable
circumstances, have been welcomed by the Jewish minority
he had oppressed so fiercely. However, as the winter of 1216
approached, the future of English Jewry, as well as that of the
kingdom itself, was anything but certain and far from secure.

3

Jewish Life and Lending in the Twelfth and Thirteenth Centuries

It is worth pausing at this point in the chronological account to consider what ordinary life might have been like for England's Jews during the time they spent in England before 1290. This is a difficult task because the bulk of the evidence which survives, whilst abundant, tends to be overwhelmingly official and technical in both tone and content. It is also one-sided in that it was produced largely by the government rather than by the Jews themselves. The rolls of the Exchequer and the Chancery, and the plea rolls of the Exchequer of the Jews give only glimpses of the everyday lives of English Jews after 1066. And beyond the extensive records of the royal administration,

the chroniclers are often unhelpful because of their prejudice;
and when they do mention individual Jews, they inevitably
focus on the sensational rather than the mundane. It was noted
over a hundred years ago how difficult it was 'to realise what
a medieval English Jew was in the moments when he was not
lending money, making payments to the king's exchequer, or
being plundered and massacred'.[1] And although a wealth of new
evidence has been studied and published since these comments
were made, and although new questions continue to be asked of
the old evidence as well, they remain frustratingly valid.

Nevertheless, some sort of analysis can still be made. It
is generally accepted, for example, that England's Jewish
community as a whole was always relatively small. Some near-
contemporary chroniclers estimated that there were as many as
17,000 Jews in England at the time of the Expulsion in 1290.[2]
However, modern commentators have been reluctant to accept
this figure. It has been suggested that there might have been as
few as 2,500–3,000 Jews in England in 1290 and that, even in
the first few decades of the thirteenth century, when English
Jewry was probably at its maximum size, it is unlikely that it
contained more than 5,000 members. England's Jews thus made
up a very small proportion of a total population of perhaps 2–4
million in 1200.[3] They were also widely spread. As has been seen,
the records of the receipts of the Northampton *donum* of 1194
show that contributions were made to the tax by members of
twenty-one separate Jewish communities. And four years earlier,
before the pogroms of 1190, there had been as many as twenty-
four provincial Jewries in the kingdom.[4] This contrasts with the
eleven communities which are known to have contributed to
the earlier *donum* of 1159.[5] However, there are some similarities
between the lists. The bulk of the settlements remained in the
south and south-east of England, although by 1194 there were
communities established as far west as Hereford and Exeter. The
London Jewry made the biggest contribution to both taxes,

although the proportion of the total paid by London in 1194
(about a third) was significantly smaller than in 1159 (about two-
thirds). The other main communities by and large had held their
positions, too. Winchester, Lincoln, Cambridge, Northampton
and Oxford all made sizeable contributions to both taxes. By
1194, however, there had been some changes. Thetford and
Bungay, for example, both important contributors to the *donum*
of 1159, do not appear on the records for 1194; perhaps the anti-
Jewish risings of 1190 in East Anglia also brought their existence
to an end. And other communities appear to have become well
established by then; at Canterbury, for example, where the Jews
are credited with a payment of over £242, the third largest of
all in 1194, exceeded only by Lincoln and London. Indeed, the
largest individual contribution to the tax (£115 6s 8d) was made
by Jacob of Canterbury. Other inferences can be drawn from
the records of 1194, too. At Norwich, for example, the Jewish
community made the second largest contribution to the *donum*
of 1159, but it was well down the list in eighth place in 1194.
Perhaps this was also a reflection of the difficulties that community had faced in 1190. And the most obvious absentee from
the list of receipts from 1194 was York. No contributions to the
donum were recorded as having been received from England's
northernmost Jewry. After the pogrom of 1190, little had been
done to re-establish a meaningful Jewish presence there.

Having said all this, it is unlikely that all of England's Jews
were town-dwellers, and recent research has suggested that
there may have been Jewish communities in smaller villages
and settlements across the kingdom.[6] Nevertheless, the numbers involved here would inevitably have been small, and most
English Jews would have lived in towns in order to be near the
local castle and, where there was one, the local mint. Most Jews,
too, would have lived in a town with its own *archa* so as to make
their business transactions more straightforward. Even then,
with approximately 5,000 men, women and children spread

across twenty or so major settlements, the number of Jews living
in any one place in 1200 was bound to be small. Once again,
confident estimates are not possible because the evidence is so
unyielding. Nevertheless, it has been suggested that, London
apart, no major English provincial Jewry (York or Lincoln, for
example) would have had more than 200–300 inhabitants; and
most of the other Jewries would have contained no more than
100–200 inhabitants.[7] And if the contributions made to royal
taxes are probably reasonably reliable indicators of the relative
size and wealth of individual Jewish communities, the contributions made by individual Jews to a local Jewry's total payment
probably reflected the status of those individuals within that
community. Jacob of Canterbury has already been mentioned
as having paid nearly half of the sum received from that town.
In London in 1194, the lead was taken by Deulesault Episcopus
(nearly £98, a fifth of the London total), Josce son of Isaac (£53)
and Benedict Parvus (£51). And two London women, Abigail
and Muriel, also made significant contributions, £40 7s 8d and
£21 3s 4d respectively. Of the twenty-one largest individual
contributions made to the 1194 tax, eight were from London,
five from Lincoln, two from Canterbury and one each from
Gloucester, Norwich, Northampton, Winchester, Cambridge
and Oxford.

But if they were widely dispersed, contact between the different Jewish communities in England was almost certainly regular
and frequent. Jews travelled for reasons of religion and business
and in order to maintain family links, and sometimes they did
so in unlikely company. For example, Gerald of Wales told a
story about a Jew who travelled to Shrewsbury in company
with the dean and archdeacon of that town.[8] Such mobility,
however, was certainly something the king was keen to control. In 1237, for example, the sheriff of Northamptonshire was
ordered to ensure that no Jew in his shire lived outside the
town of Northampton itself. And in 1239, the king ordered that

wherever any Jew was at Michaelmas in that year, he should stay there with his family for the following year.[9] Indeed, by the 1230s, it seems to have been the case that Jews were actually obliged to live in one of the towns in which *archae* had been set up for the registration of Jewish debts. When the system of Jewish debt registration had been instituted in 1194, *archae* were opened in only six or seven towns.[10] It is likely, though, that this number was soon found to have been too small, and by the start of Henry III's reign, seventeen towns had their own *archae*. These were Bristol, Cambridge, Canterbury, Colchester, Exeter, Gloucester, Hereford, Lincoln, London, Northampton, Norwich, Nottingham, Oxford, Stamford, Winchester, Worcester and York. The restrictive royal orders of the 1230s were clear signs of the increasingly oppressive regime that England's Jews were living under by that decade. It should also be said, however, that the fact that similar orders were issued repeatedly after this point might suggest that they were not easy to enforce. Perhaps England's medieval Jews moved around the kingdom more freely than the records allow us to know.

Within their settlements, the Jews did not live apart from the Christian majority. They were certainly not forced by law to live in ghettos, behind walls or within other prescribed zones, and they would have lived side by side with Christians, and talked and socialised with them in many places. It has been said that 'left to themselves [Jews and Gentiles] got on well enough together', and that whilst there were often times when the relationships between them fractured or broke down completely, 'we should not overlook the interludes of gruff cordiality'.[11] Sometimes, indeed, Jews appeared in what might at first sight seem to have been the most incongruous of places. According to Jocelin of Brakelond, for example, at the abbey of Bury St Edmunds in the 1170s and early 1180s, the Jews of the town 'had free entrance and exit, and went everywhere throughout the monastery, wandering by the altars and round the shrine while

Mass was being celebrated'.[12] They may have looked different, of
course, but it is impossible to be sure about this. Contemporary
depictions of Jews often show them wearing distinctive headgear, in particular the pointed *pileum cornutum* hat, and as having
hook noses, beards and curly forelocks. They are often shown
wearing a hooded cloak, too, although there may not have been
anything distinctively 'Jewish' about this. And in any event, these
are usually hostile caricatures, and the true extent of any physical differences between medieval Jews and Christians cannot
reliably be gauged from them. According to excavations undertaken at the medieval Jewish cemetery in York in the early 1980s,
England's medieval Jews appear to have been slightly shorter
than their Christian contemporaries; and the shapes of their
skulls showed differences, too. That Jewish women appear to
have lived longer and that Jewish infant mortality rates appear
to have been lower than in Christian communities have also
been interpreted as evidence of better standards of medical care
within the Jewish community and of higher nutritional and
hygiene standards in Jewish families than in Christian ones. Jews
certainly tended to wash more regularly than their Christian
neighbours – they were required to do so on waking, before
praying and eating and after carrying out their bodily functions.
Women, too, were expected to immerse themselves totally once
a month.[13] Whatever physical differences there were, however,
it is hard to know whether they were particularly noticeable to
the casual observer. The popular belief that Jews had a distinctive smell (*foetor judaicus*), for example, must have been based
on hostile prejudice rather than objective reality. It served both
to associate Jews with the Devil, who was reputed to have his
own unique odour of brimstone and sulphur, and to distinguish
them from Christian saints who characteristically smelt sweet
and fragrant long after death.[14]

More concretely, the thirteenth century was also to see
repeated attempts by the royal government to enforce the

wearing of the tabula by Jewish men and women. There are
several images in contemporary English sources showing Jewish
men wearing this distinguishing symbol.[15] But generally, it is
not clear quite how distinctive the appearance of Jews tended
to be. It is certainly possible to argue (indeed, this was the
justification used at the Fourth Lateran Council in 1215 which
tried to enforce the wearing of the tabula) that the wearing of
special clothing was necessary because, without such identifying
marks, it was difficult to tell Jews and their Christian neighbours
apart. Everyday contacts between Christians and Jews were perhaps seen as so dangerous 'because they were so normal'.[16] The
repeated attempts by the Church and the government during
the thirteenth century to ban Christian women acting as servants in Jewish households, as midwives at Jewish births or as wet
nurses to Jewish children clearly imply that such practices were
relatively commonplace. As late as 1286, Christians were invited
to a Jewish wedding in Hereford, an event which outraged
the local bishop. He stipulated that all who had attended the
celebration should receive absolution within eight days or face
excommunication.[17] It was the great fear of the ecclesiastical
authorities that, if Christians were exposed for too long to Jewish
ideas and beliefs, they might succumb to them and stray from
the Christian path. Jews had been viewed with suspicion since
Roman times partly because of their active proselytising. And
sometimes conversions did occur, although often in the context
of a relationship that had developed between a Jewish woman
and a Christian man. In 1222, for example, a deacon converted
to Judaism and went so far as to circumcise himself because he
fell in love with a Jewish woman. He was burnt outside the walls
of Oxford.[18] And in 1275, a Dominican friar, Robert of Reading,
died in prison after marrying a Jewish woman and being circumcised. Such cases cannot have been common, however (the
fact that Robert of Reading appeared before Edward I himself
before being handed over to the ecclesiastical authorities to be

dealt with shows this), and they came to be recorded precisely because they were unusual and notorious.[19]

But even though they might mix sometimes unobtrusively with their Gentile neighbours, English Jews still formed a separate and exclusive community. As such, they were obvious targets for suspicion and misunderstanding. They ate different food, spoke different languages, had their own customs and observances and educated their children apart from the Christian majority. And although in theory they could live anywhere within a particular town or city, they tended to live together in areas (a street, perhaps, or, in the bigger communities, a number of streets) which would have been recognised by Jews and Christians alike as the local Jewry. Within each Jewry, community life centred on the synagogue or *schola Iudeorum*. There may have been more than one in a particular settlement, and these would have varied in size. Some synagogues would have been no more than rooms in the houses of prominent local Jews, and some of these may have been intended for private family use only. Others would have been separate buildings in their own right, perhaps attached to or adjoining the house of one of the wealthy Jewish patrons who were obliged to pay for the synagogue's upkeep. As has been seen, for example, the Great Synagogue of the London Jewry, originally established by Rabbi Josce in the early twelfth century, was situated on the eastern side of Colechurch Lane off Cheapside.[20] And the synagogue which survives at Lincoln remains an imposing stone building which would almost certainly have dominated its immediate surroundings. Other synagogues were probably more discreet and constructed out of sight to avoid confrontation and deter attack.[21] Wherever they were positioned, these buildings performed various functions. The word 'synagogue' in fact simply means 'place of assembly', and there communal meetings would have been held and announcements made. Indeed, it was in the synagogue that royal pronouncements concerning the Jews would have been read out.[22] However, in addition to this, and as well as housing the local community's *mikvah* or ritual bath, the synagogues were primarily places of prayer and study. After all, 'Jewish education and religion were clearly paramount in Jewish social life'.[23] Jewish children were taught the basic tenets of their faith in the synagogue, and 'the extraordinary Jewish emphasis on education' continued into later life, where at least some degree of literacy was required for Jewish men to take part in the synagogue services as they were expected to do every morning and evening.[24] Indeed, it is likely that many if not most of England's Jews would have been able to read, write and speak three and perhaps even four different languages (Latin, Norman-French, Hebrew and English), although their preferred first language for everyday transactions and conversation would probably have been Norman-French. Of course, though, which language was ultimately used would depend to a large extent on the social status of a particular client. A high-status borrower would probably not be spoken to in the same language as someone from a less exalted social group.[25] The important point here, however, is that Jews were educated to a standard unknown to most of their Christian neighbours, and at the higher levels of study, it has been said that English medieval Jewry was 'a hive of productive rabbinic scholarship'. Under the patronage of men such as Jurnet of Norwich, his son Isaac and Isaac's own two sons Moses and Samuel, for example, scholarly life in Norwich flourished in the half-century after 1190.[26]

It was clearly possible, therefore, and probably even desirable, for intellectual activity such as this to take place within the family. Other details about Jewish family life in medieval England are few and far between, however. It is not even possible to state with confidence whether Jewish families tended to be large or small. It has been taken as a 'reasonably well established fact' that most would not have been large or extended, and that parents with more than three or four children would have been the exception rather than the rule. The excavations at York suggested that Jewish women tended to live longer than their Christian counterparts, and it has been suggested that, as well as having a better diet and general standards of hygiene, perhaps this was because they encountered the perils of childbirth less frequently. There is evidence which shows, however, that Jewish families could be large, and generalisations are not likely to be helpful.[27]

Heavily involved in the life and business affairs of England's medieval Jewish community, however, were its women. The extent of that involvement is now under closer study than ever before, and the results are already arresting. Jewish marriages were usually arranged by the parents, although the preferences of the young couple involved would probably be taken into account. Moreover, it was open to the bride to break off the match if she decided that her intended partner was unsuitable in some way. If the marriage went ahead, however, according to the Jewish scholar Maimonides (1135–1204), there were certain things that a newly married Jewish couple should have. A *ketuba* or dowry should be provided at the start of the marriage; officially in England this appears to have been £100 (although this must have been beyond the financial reach of many ordinary Jews), half from the bride or her family, half from the groom or his relations. In addition, a Jewish wife was entitled to her own lavatory and a monthly visit to her parents. And she was not obliged simply to submit to her husband's sexual demands.[28] How far such ideals were met in practice is difficult to say; there were Jewish divorces in England between 1066 and 1290, so not every marriage can have proceeded harmoniously. It is becoming increasingly clear, however, that in many ways Jewish women enjoyed more freedom and room for independent action than their Christian counterparts. In the strict eyes of the law, they were on terms of 'complete legal sexual equality' with Jewish men.[29] Jewish women were able to hold property in their own right before they were widowed. If her husband was a lender, a wife could act on his behalf in making and recording a loan. She could lend on her own account, too, as well as taking an active part in her husband's business. Suzanne Bartlet has found evidence in the records of the Jewish Exchequer which shows more than forty women dealing in loans or linked transactions during the thirteenth century.[30] It has also been suggested that women may have taken the major role in the pledging of items for small sums of money, pawnbroking in other words; an activity which, because of the relative triviality of the individual amounts involved, tends to leave little trace in the records. Jewish widows, like Christian ones, were entitled to be supported out of their deceased husband's estates; some would also try to carry on the family business themselves.[31] That two London Jewesses, Abigail and Muriel, made significant contributions to the *donum* of 1194, shows how important they could be, and how they could be involved with large sums as well as small.[32] And Bartlet's work on the careers of Chera, Belia and Licoricia, three Jewish business-women from thirteenth-century Winchester, has revealed the prominence of the roles they played in both local and national affairs. The story of Licoricia of Winchester in particular, as well as containing the details of the life and business activities of one of the richest women in England, has all the elements of a soap opera. She became the wife of the great financier David of Oxford in the early 1240s, but only after David had scandal-ously divorced his previous wife, Muriel. On David's death in 1244 Henry III allowed Licoricia to take over his business in return for a payment of £3,333. This made her 'an extremely wealthy woman', and thereafter she appears to have run the business in association with her sons. Not without difficulty, however. She was tallaged heavily by the royal government and she was imprisoned in the late 1250s having been accused of stealing a valuable ring which was on its way to Henry III himself. In 1277, she was found stabbed to death in her Winchester home.[33] Much more research into the lives and careers of Jewish women is required, but it does seem right to say that 'the female members of the Jewish community were of more critical importance to the relations between Christians and Jews than has ever been allowed'.[34] It would be wrong, however, to suppose from this that all Jewish women were heavily involved in finance; some were and some were not. And ultimately, Jewish men and women saw themselves as having different but closely linked primary responsibilities towards their communities and their families: 'the one was supreme in the synagogue and the house of study, the other was supreme in the house, and it is wrong to think of the latter as being inferior to the former'.[35]

Another local focus for Jewish life would have been the cemetery. Until 1177, there was only one Jewish burial ground, or 'Jews' Garden' as they were often referred to, in England, and that was in London, outside the walls of the city at Cripplegate. Jews from all over England would have been brought there for burial.[36] Thomas of Monmouth, for example, described how the body of one Norwich Jew, Eleazar, was carried from Norwich to London in about 1146.[37] In 1177, however, presumably because the Jewish population in England had expanded so significantly by that time, the king allowed the Jews to have a cemetery outside the walls of every city in England.[38] The fledgling York community had soon established its own cemetery north-west of the city walls in the area still known as Jewbury. Other Jewries were not as quick to act. The new burial ground at York was originally shared with the communities at Lincoln and Northampton, although these Jewries acquired their own cemeteries later. Ultimately, Jewish cemeteries were also established at Norwich, Oxford, Winchester, Bristol, Cambridge and Canterbury.

During their 200 years or so in England before 1290, it was possible to find Jews performing a wide range of activities. Every major lender would have had his staff of assistants and clerks, for example. There are several examples of Jewish goldsmiths, too, and even more Jewish physicians, some of whom at least may have served beyond the limits of their own communities. There were dangers in professing to have medical skills, however, especially if something went wrong and blame needed to be apportioned. There was a fine line in the contemporary Christian imagination between medicine and witchcraft, and such an association only served to strengthen the widely held view that Jews were both poisoners and magicians. There are other glimpses of intriguing individuals, as well: in Norwich, Diaia le Scalarius ('the ladder-maker'), for example, and at Gloucester, Abraham le Skirmiseur ('the fencing-master'). And at the more grisly end of the employment spectrum, it seems that King John at least was not averse to using Jews as torturers and executioners.[39] It was John, too, who granted a house in Canterbury in 1215 to 'the Jew, Abraham the Crossbowman'.[40] Despite this apparent diversity, however, it is probably right to say that 'in England, Jewish non-financial business seems to have been of peripheral importance'.[41] Of course, this is not the same as saying that all Jews lent money on an extensive scale; Colin Richmond has estimated that Jewish financiers themselves numbered no more than one in a hundred of the total Jewish population.[42] If this is correct, then there can never have been more than fifty or so such men. And indeed, within the Jewish community, there were always certain great men who dominated affairs, Aaron of Lincoln in the late twelfth century, for example, and Aaron of York and David of Oxford in the first half of the thirteenth. Nevertheless, it is probably fair to say that most of England's Jews would have been involved in some way in the business of providing credit, whether by making smaller loans less often than their more illustrious leaders, or by working for lenders in some capacity or other. After all, it has been suggested that 'the majority of Jewish households in every English

community for which there are adequate records had at least
a little money out on loan, even if only a few pounds'.[43] And,
indeed, it was its vast lending capacity which gave the Jews of
twelfth- and thirteenth-century England an importance belied
by their mere numbers. It has been estimated, for example,
that the total wealth of England's Jewish population in the
early 1240s (something, it bears repeating, between 3,000 and
5,000 men, women and children or about 1.25 per cent of the
kingdom's urban population) was approximately £133,333, or
'about a third of the total circulating coin in England at that
time'.[44] Nevertheless, it would be a mistake to assume that all
of England's medieval Jews were rich or well-off. Inevitably,
many were poor and had to make their living as best they
could. Indeed, it has been suggested that 'at all times the vast
majority of Jews were poor, and in many cases miserably so'.[45]
Given that such lifestyles were of little interest either to the
government or the chroniclers, however, it is almost impossible
to find conclusive evidence about this. It has been estimated in
the case of Norwich, however, that poor Jews made up as much
as a third of the Jewish population there (about fifty out of
perhaps 150 people) in the first half of the twelfth century.[46]

It has already been seen in Chapter 1 how the Jews established
themselves in England after 1066 as traders in plate and bullion,
and how they had come to concentrate on moneylending by
the close of the twelfth century. It is now appropriate to look a
little more closely at how the system of Jewish lending operated
by the thirteenth century. Usury, as has been seen, was a sin in
the eyes of the Christian Church. And in the century and a half
following the Council of Tours' prohibition of the practice, the
Church's views only hardened further. By the early fourteenth
century, usury was regarded as a form of heresy and 'the usurer
was ranked with witches, robbers, fornicators and adulterers. The
sin of usury and avarice came to be classed as equally as serious as
homicide, sacrilege, perjury, incest and homosexuality. The usurer

himself was to be an outcast'.[47] Nevertheless, in spite of such views, usury was generally tolerated as a distasteful yet necessary fact of ordinary commercial life and everyday existence in the twelfth and thirteenth centuries. Christians were not supposed to lend money, but some did. It has already been explained why there were probably few English Christian usurers by 1200, but thirteenth-century Englishmen would still have been able to find Lombard, Cahorsin and Italian financiers who were prepared to advance them funds if the repayment terms were acceptable. Indeed, as the financial predicament of England's Jews worsened during the thirteenth century, such alternatives had to be found by many of those English Gentiles accustomed to living on credit.

In the first half of the thirteenth century at least, however, there can be little doubt that the English market in money-lending was dominated by Jewish practitioners. And despite the Church's disapproval, the royal government had given its seal of approval to the activities of such men when it set up the system for the registration of Jewish debts in the aftermath of the massacres of 1189–90. Of course, the scrupulous and prudent Christian who was lent money by a Jewish lender would still have been keen to avoid any suggestion that he was practising usury, or at the very least to conceal any usurious element in a particular transaction; and there were various ways of doing this.[48] In the documents detailing the terms of the loan, for example, the interest might have been concealed within the principal sum lent. In other words, the agreement might state that the borrower received £10, whereas in reality the loan was for £9 and an extra £1 was payable in interest when the repayment fell due. Only the lender and the borrower would therefore know the true nature of the transaction. Another way of making a profit was to include a penalty clause or *lucrum* at the end of an agreement. If the loan was not repaid when due, the debtor would incur a financial penalty. And it was also possible to lend money and stipulate repayment in terms of goods or commodities. There was a risk for the lender in this, however; if he was to be repaid in crops, for example, he might end up recovering less than the amount he had lent in the first place.

Allegations of usury might be avoided altogether if money was borrowed in return for some sort of valuable security. Such security could take any form, except for bloodstained clothing (which might have been obtained by violence) and items used in church services.[49] The Assize of Arms of 1181 also stated that Jews had immediately to sell coats of mail which came into their possession, 'that they may continue to be in the king's service'.[50] Strikingly, too, 'it would be hard to exaggerate the extent to which, despite official ecclesiastical prohibition, Bibles, chalices, church ornaments, and other items central to the practice of the Christian religion were regularly pledged to members (often female) of the English provincial Jewries'. Jocelin of Brakelond, indeed, described how, at Bury St Edmunds in the second half of the twelfth century, 'silk copes, gold vessels and other church ornaments were often pawned without the consent of the convent'.[51] But by far the most popular, because most valuable, form of security was land. There were two ways of making such an arrangement. First, during the term of the loan, the lender would hold the land and take the profits from it. If the loan was repaid in full and on time, the borrower would get the land back. Alternatively, the land would become the creditor's own possession when the loan was contracted, but the debtor would continue to take the profits from it until the loan was repaid. In both cases, of course, if the borrower defaulted, his land and its profits were forfeit to the lender. And if it became clear to the borrower before payment was due that he was not going to be able to repay the loan, he might seek the help of another interested party who would pay off the loan and in return receive the land from the lender. Either way, for the debtor who borrowed on the security of land, the stakes were high and the risks were serious.

Where interest was payable on a loan, and where it is possible to see it being charged, rates tended to be high. Aaron of Lincoln had charged interest at the rate of one, two or three pence in the pound weekly, and such rates were probably not unusual. Royal legislation in 1233 and 1239 attempted to limit the amount of interest charged to a maximum of 2d per pound per week (43.5 per cent per annum), but whilst this brings up interesting issues about the English government's attitude towards the Church's policies on usury, it is hard to know how strictly such restrictions were adhered to.[52] Interest would have been payable from the beginning of the loan, or as a lump sum at the end of the term. And just as Aaron of Lincoln's interest rates appear to have been representative, so does his client base. Most of Aaron's loans appear to have been made to men of relatively low standing; but most of his money was lent to a small number of high-status individuals, knights and barons, or religious houses. And such a pattern was repeated by Aaron's successors across England; for 'without denying that the numerical majority of Jewish loans in England were for small sums advanced to peasants and townsmen, the fact remains that, prior to 1275, the great bulk of Jewish capital in England was committed to loans of £10 or more made to the socially eminent... The Jews of England, then, made the great bulk of their profits from large loans to very great men'.[53] This was certainly the case in mid-thirteenth-century Hereford, as Joe Hillaby has shown. There were more knights and freeholders than barons who owed money to the financier Hamo of Hereford in 1244, but it was the barons who owed 83 per cent of the sums involved. Over £2,150 of the £2,500 or so owing to Hamo in that year had been borrowed by only six great landholders of the southern Welsh March.[54] Nevertheless, it is still important to bear in mind the variety and range of the Jewish lenders' clientele. A wide range of social groups across the kingdom were involved with Jewish creditors. In Norwich in the 1220s, for example, most of those indebted to the Jews were 'members of the rural gentry'; and only a small number of debts were owed by barons or religious houses.[55] Similarly, in Cambridgeshire in the thirteenth century, 'well over seventy per cent of Jewish debtors belonged to the agricultural classes, and particularly to the smaller tenants'.[56]

However, the two groups whose dealings with the Jews have received most attention are the knights and the religious houses. The former will be discussed a little more fully in the next chapter, but it is worth dwelling on the Jews' ecclesiastical clients here. It may seem strange, given the Church's hostile views about the Jews and their commercial activities, that so many religious houses borrowed money from them and transacted in Jewish debts. The fact is, however, that without such involvement, many monasteries would never have become as rich and powerful as they eventually did. From at least the late twelfth century, for example, the Cistercian abbey of Meaux in the East Riding of Yorkshire had been active in the land market with the help of Jewish financiers. Several other Cistercian abbeys in the county also owed debts totalling more than £4,000 to Aaron of Lincoln when he died in 1186.[57] They may have taken out loans with which to build, buy land or sheep (the mainstay of Cistercian wealth), but it is much more likely that these sums were owed because the monasteries had taken over the debts of others in return for the land which secured the loans. Indeed, the appetite for Jewish finance amongst the Cistercian monasteries of Yorkshire played no small part in restoring the fortunes of the York Jewry after the calamity of 1190, and in making it, by the 1240s, the richest provincial Jewry in England.[58] Such activities were by no means confined to the Cistercians of Yorkshire, however. Many religious orders, of both men and women, were involved in similar transactions, and examples can be found from across England. The monks at Canterbury, Westminster, Norwich and Gloucester are all known to have been involved with Jewish lenders.[59]

After reviewing the evidence, one historian concluded that 'it is obviously impossible to say how much land was acquired by religious houses by means of transactions in encumbered estates, but it is safe to infer that the practice was widespread and general'.[60] But a monastery's involvement with Jewish lending was not always a sign of its entrepreneurial skill or business acumen. At Bury St Edmunds in the late twelfth century, for example, indebtedness to the Jews became a fact of monastic life as a result of poor management. Jocelin of Brakelond painted a vivid picture of how the weak leadership of Abbot Hugh allowed individuals within the abbey community to borrow without authorisation and so plunge it into debt. These debts were a constant source of concern for Hugh's successor, Abbot Samson.[61]

The Jews of medieval England thus spent their time trying to balance the different demands placed upon them. But because they were an exclusive and distinctive group in both religious and cultural terms, this was never easy. They had to practise their own religion and follow their own customs; this inevitably set them apart from their Christian neighbours and made them targets for hostility. At the same time as they wished to maintain their separateness, however, they were also bound to interact with the Christian world around them if they were to carry on their business activities and retain any kind of protection from persecution. As a vulnerable and exposed minority, tolerated only grudgingly at best, the threat of violence and impoverishment must have been one with which all medieval English Jews lived daily.

4

King Henry III
and the Assault on
England's Jews

The coronation of Henry III took place on 28 October
1216 at Gloucester. The new king was a boy of just
nine, and his new kingdom was in turmoil. Louis, the
eldest son of the king of France, was in England and in control
of London; hence Henry's coronation taking place far from
Westminster Abbey. Louis also had the allegiance of a majority
of England's greatest barons. However, Henry's claim to the
throne was safeguarded by a regency council led by William
Marshal, Earl of Pembroke, the respected elder statesman of
the English nobility, and by the papal legate Guala. In order
to obtain papal support in his struggle against his rebellious
barons, King John had made England a papal fief. Thus, the
Pope, Honorius III, had become the feudal overlord of the
young English king and, with papal authority in his hands,

Guala was able to undermine Prince Louis's cause by excommunicating him and by turning the struggle against him into a crusade. Louis could find no English bishop who was prepared to crown him king.

Perilous though his situation was in 1216, therefore, Henry III's cause was by no means a lost one. In a bid to generate more support, the members of the regency council reissued Magna Carta in November 1216, albeit with some of the more controversial clauses from the original charter of the previous year, including even the mild restrictions on the administration of Jewish debts contained in chapters 10 and 11, omitted. And they took Louis on in battle, too. The crucial stronghold of Dover Castle, control of which led to command over the English Channel, was defended magnificently for Henry by Hubert de Burgh. Then, on 20 May 1217, Louis's forces were defeated at Lincoln; and, on 24 August, a French fleet bringing reinforcements was destroyed off Sandwich by Hubert de Burgh. Under the terms of the Treaty of Kingston-Lambeth of September 1217, Louis agreed to abandon his claims to the English throne and he returned to France. In November 1217, Magna Carta, sealed by Guala and the Marshal, was reissued once more. England had been kept out of French hands, but only just. And there was still much work to be done by the representatives of the young king.[1]

The position of England's Jews was considered by the new government in 1218, in the aftermath of the Fourth Lateran Council which had taken place late in 1215.[2] The council had issued various restrictive decrees concerning the Jews, the intention of which amongst other things had been to restrict Jewish lending, to compel Jews to pay tithes and other ecclesiastical dues and to limit contact between Jews and Gentiles. With England under papal authority at this time, and with a papal legate in control of the administration, it is hardly surprising that England was the first place where the practical application

of these restrictions was debated. Interestingly, though, most of
the decrees of 1215 were not implemented. At a great council
held at Westminster in May 1218, it was decided that the Jews
of England should continue to enjoy the same privileges as
they had in previous reigns. The right of the provincial Jewries
to govern themselves according to their own laws, which had
first been conceded by Henry II, albeit with some reservations
to preserve royal rights, was confirmed.[3] And well aware of
its own financial weakness and of the funds the Jews might
provide, the regency government confirmed that the Jews
would still be protected by royal officials. Special instructions
were even sent to Gloucester, Lincoln, Bristol and Oxford
ordering that Jews should be shielded from attack, particularly
by prospective crusaders.[4] The new papal legate, Pandulph,
was not happy with the favourable treatment received by
the English Jews at the hands of their royal protector; he was
particularly outraged by the conduct of Isaac of Norwich,
England's wealthiest Jew at this time.[5] Nevertheless, the only
concession made by the royal government to ecclesiastical feeling came in March 1218 with the adoption of another of the
conciliar decrees: henceforth, all Jews were ordered to wear
a distinguishing badge. Two rectangles of parchment or white
textile, each with a rounded top, were to be sewn on to clothing. The carefully prescribed design was intended to represent
the two tablets (*tabula*) of the Mosaic Law.[6] This was seen
as necessary to prevent unwitting contact (particularly sexual
contact) between Jews and Christians and it was, of course, an
ominous development. But, initially at least, there is little reason
to think that the new rule was intended specifically to shame
or disparage the Jews; nor does it appear to have been strictly
enforced. Exemptions could be bought either by individuals
or whole communities; the Jews of Canterbury paid 8s 4d for
communal licence not to wear the badge, whilst the London
community paid 13s. Indeed, 'the dispensations granted by

1221 had been so numerous and general that very few seem
to have been required thereafter'. And until 1253, when there
was a significant change in the royal attitude towards the Jews,
'no Jew, rich or poor, need unwillingly wear the badge'.[7]

The way in which the new rules concerning the tabula
were enforced gives some indication of the relatively relaxed
way in which the Jews of England were treated in the early
decades of Henry III's reign. Indeed, the 1220s and 1230s have
been described as 'comparatively halcyon years' for English
Jewry.[8] Many Jews may have left England after the events of
1210 and others may have followed them during the civil war
of 1215–16. England's Jewish community in the early years of
Henry III's reign was almost certainly a depleted one. If so,
then the government would have been keen to persuade those
who had left to return; perhaps something of a fresh start was
envisaged. In 1218, for example, the Wardens of the Cinque
Ports were ordered to allow Jews to enter the kingdom; they
were only required to give a guarantee that they would reg-
ister themselves at the Jewish Exchequer.[9] The Jews were also
not particularly hard-pressed by the demands of royal taxation
in the 1220s and 1230s. In 1221, the English Jews contributed between £666 and £1,000 towards an aid to marry the
king's sister, Joan, to the king of Scots. Then, in 1223, they
were ordered to pay a tallage of £2,000. In 1225–6, another
assessment of £4,000 was made and in 1229 a further tallage
of £5,333 was imposed in connection with a planned royal
campaign in Brittany. A much larger tallage, of £6,666, was
imposed on the Jewish community in 1232, although payment
in instalments was later permitted. Two other smaller tallages
of £2,000 each were also imposed in 1236–7. The financial
burden placed by the royal government on the Jews, therefore,
was by no means insignificant (something between £1,000
and £2,000 per year from 1221 until 1239), but it was, by later
standards, supportable and relatively modest. It is impossible to

know what proportion of these tallages was actually paid; but given the overall wealth of the Jewish community in England at this time, it is likely that the bulk of the obligations was discharged.[10]

It was in the late 1230s and early 1240s that royal policy towards the Jews began to harden. It is impossible to know for sure what prompted this shift in approach. However, events in France, not for the last time, may have had an influence on Henry III's attitude. In the decade or so after 1223, a series of anti-Jewish measures had been enacted by the government of the young French king, Louis IX. These culminated in 1234 with the confiscation of Jewish goods and debts, and in 1235 with the outright outlawry of Jewish usury within the royal lands. The latter was 'the first such royal order in medieval Europe'.[11] England's Jews may therefore have fallen victim to a growth in anti-Jewish feeling during the 1230s which extended far beyond England itself. To be sure, within England the strength of that feeling was obvious. The Jews were expelled from Leicester by Simon de Montfort in 1231, for example. This was presented as a pious move by Montfort, for the good of his own soul, and as an act designed to relieve the burgesses of Leicester of the weight of usury. Newcastle and Warwick also expelled their Jewish communities in 1234, High Wycombe in 1235 and Southampton in 1236.[12] Moreover, in 1232, Henry III had established the *Domus Conversorum* ('House of Converts') in London (in what is now Chancery Lane) to house those Jews who had abandoned their faith and converted to Christianity.[13] King Henry was a particularly keen supporter of Jewish conversion; he witnessed baptisms himself, frequently chose new names for the converts and organised their financial support either through the *Domus* or the religious houses to which converts might also be sent. It is not surprising, therefore, given this level of royal enthusiasm and participation, that Jewish conversions to Christianity appear to

have peaked in England during Henry's reign. There might be
many other reasons, however, why an individual Jew decided
to convert: genuine religious feeling and fear of persecution
were the most likely. But as Stacey has shown, 'the upsurge
in conversions between 1240 and 1260 reflects the corrosive effect of Henry III's excessive royal taxation of the Jews
during those years'.[14] More will be said about this shortly, but
mid-century poverty amongst England's Jews, along with the
inevitable decline in the Jewish community's ability to meet
the financial needs of its more desperate members, may have
persuaded many of them to convert. After all, for those converts
who ended up there, the *Domus* at least provided a secure and
stable environment. The belongings of a converted Jew were
confiscated by the crown, but residents of the *Domus* received
a weekly allowance (10d for men and 8d for women), a roof
over their heads and instruction in the true faith. They lived
as if in a monastery, notwithstanding the presence of women,
eating at communal tables, studying and worshipping together.
The *Domus* was designed to prepare Jewish converts for their
new life as practising Christians and its establishment was a sure
sign that the king (Henry had a reputation as 'the most pious
king' after all) had not given up hope of eventually bringing
all his Jewish subjects back into the Christian fold.[15]

It has also been suggested that what happened between
1239 and 1241 served as punishment of the Jews for some
crime in which they were alleged to have been involved and
of which no reliable record survives.[16] It is possible that it was
in part a reaction to events which had occurred at Norwich
in 1234, when the Jewish community there was accused of
having seized and forcibly circumcised a boy, possibly the son
of a converted Jew, four years previously. Riots took place
and Jewish houses were burned, whilst some of the accused
were either executed or outlawed. These incidents were followed by another issue of the royal prohibition on Christian

women working for Jews as nurses or servants. In any event,
in 1239, when echoes of the Norwich case were still being
heard, the royal government demanded of the Jews a third
of the value of all their goods and debts.[17] Unfortunately, the
sources do not allow any confident estimate of the amount
collected by the government as a result of this order. However,
it seems probable that the receipts were disappointing; perhaps
the tax raised no more than £3,000. And it may have been
its unhappiness with the results of the third of 1239, as well
as a suspicion that many Jews had evaded payment, which
prompted the government to enquire much more rigorously
and systematically into Jewish wealth in 1240–1. In June 1240,
the king ordered the closure of the *archae* across England and
at about the same time an attempt was made to compile an
accurate census of all the Jews in England aged twelve or more.
Then, in January 1241, representatives from every Jewish community in England were summoned to gather at Worcester
in February to arrange the collection of a tallage of £13,333,
easily the largest such tax since 1210. It was needed to finance
the king's planned expedition to Poitou, which took place in
1242. The Jews were given a year in which to pay and, unlike
in 1239–40, they did not drag their feet. The surviving records
show that nearly £9,000 was certainly collected in response
to the 1241 order, and the actual receipts may have been more
considerable still. Nearly half of this amount came from York
(£4,485 18s 1d), a strong indication of how successfully that
city's Jewish community had re-established itself after the horrors of 1190, and of the dominant place it held at the centre
of Jewish affairs in England by the 1240s. Nearly 22 per cent
came from London (£1,503 13s ½d) and just over 12 per cent
from Oxford (£1,150 14s). Between them, another sixteen
Jewish communities contributed the balance. Such figures
do not tell the whole story, however. Over two-thirds of the
known receipts (approximately £6,200) were paid by only

thirteen individuals, and of this sum three men, Aaron of York, his father-in-law Leo, and David of Oxford, contributed no less than £4,700. Aaron, indeed, who was also archpresbyter of the English Jews at this time, was the wealthiest of the three (he has been described as a 'Croesus of thirteenth-century England'[18]), having made his money out of lending to the monastic houses of Yorkshire. In 1241, his estate was valued for taxation purposes at £40,000.[19] This concentration of Jewish wealth in the hands of such a small number of men is certainly 'astonishing'.[20] It was also dangerous; without them, the ability of the rest of England's Jewish community to meet the government's continuing demands would be seriously tested. And unfortunately, the tallage of 1241 was only the first in a series of swingeing royal impositions on the English Jews.

In 1244, the imposition of a further tallage of no less than £40,000 ('the heaviest in the history of the English Jews'[21]), payable over five years, was announced. By this time, both David of Oxford and Leo of York were dead, and whilst the 1241 tax had not broken them, it would certainly have reduced their reserves of cash. These reserves would have been depleted further as a result of the £8,000 which between them their heirs had had to pay into the royal coffers for the privilege of succeeding to their estates.[22] Aaron of York was the only one of the great triumvirate of 1241–2 to have survived, so the weight of the 1244 tallage may have fallen on him. By 1255, bemoaning that he had paid the royal government more than £20,000 in tallages and other sums between 1243 and 1250, he was bankrupt.[23] Unfortunately, records of the sums collected between 1244 and 1249 are fragmentary; the government's aims may simply have been too ambitious and the yield disappointing. Stacey has still observed, however, that 'the double blows of the 20,000 mark tallage of 1241–2 and the 60,000 mark tallage of 1244–50 ruined the Jewish magnates of England,

and effectively decapitated the class structure of medieval Anglo-Jewry. By so doing, Henry III broke the financial backbone of the English Jewish community, and permanently reduced its financial value to the Crown'.[24] If so, however, this did not stop further tallages being assessed: £6,666 in 1250, £3,000 in 1251 and 1252, £2,777 in 1253, £6,666 in 1254 and £1,333 in 1255. Therefore, between 1241 and 1255, nearly £67,000 in direct taxation was assessed by the royal government against the Jews of England, more than three times what had been assessed between 1221 and 1239. It is worth emphasising again that certain knowledge of how much money was actually collected is lacking, but it is has been convincingly argued that more than half of the total wealth of England's Jewry was paid to the crown in taxation between 1241 and 1256.[25]

During these years, then, England's Jewish community, which was 'per capita... almost certainly the wealthiest Jewish community in Europe' in 1241, was subjected to regular royal financial demands of unparalleled intensity.[26] The effects of this on the community as a whole were disastrous. The 1241 tallage may have used up much of the Jews' liquid capital, so a significant proportion of the later demands would probably have been met by the discounted sale of bonds, or by demanding immediate payment from debtors. Often deals were struck whereby borrowers agreed to pay less than the face value of their debt in order to provide the lender with the ready cash he needed to meet his tallage obligations. Thus the increasingly desperate measures taken by Jewish lenders to recover their debts only served to speed up their descent into penury. And the pressures placed on borrowers to pay up quickly can only have served to increase hostility towards the Jewish community as a whole. This pressure came not just from the lenders themselves, but from the government, too, which, in the end, bothered little about precisely where its Jewish funds came from. The receipt roll for the tallage of £3,333 which was due at Easter 1254 shows that, of approximately £2,666 paid, a quarter of this came directly from Christians who owed money to Jewish creditors. Such individuals were likely to blame both the Jews and the royal government for this state of affairs. But the Jews were easier targets, and so after 1240 the Jews' financial decline went hand in hand with rising Christian resentment towards them.

The mechanics and consequences of this spiralling descent into penury and abuse are worth looking at a little more closely. If a Jewish lender needed cash quickly, he might settle with a debtor for less than he was owed. Alternatively, he could sell his bonds to another lender for something less than their face value. Of course, as the financial screw tightened in the 1240s and 1250s, fewer and fewer Jewish lenders were in a position to purchase these bonds from their co-religionists; so it seems that Christian speculators were the main beneficiaries of this developing traffic in Jewish bonds. And many of these men held positions in the royal court. In 1255, for example, Stephen de Chenduit, lord of Cuxham in Oxfordshire and of Cheddington and Ibstone in Buckinghamshire, owed £55 to the Jew Abraham of Berkhampstead. Such indebtedness may partly explain why Stephen deserted his lord Richard of Cornwall in the civil war which soon followed and sided with Simon de Montfort. After all, Montfort was quick to pardon the interest on Stephen's Jewish debts. Stephen emerged from the war on the wrong side, however, and was forced to transfer his estates to Walter of Merton, the king's chancellor, in return for which Walter paid off Stephen's debts to three Lincoln Jews. Walter used his new lands to establish the Oxford college which bears his name today.[27] The king's brother, Richard of Cornwall, was another who profited from the manipulation of Jewish debts. He had a long history of dealings with the Jews, and appears to have had a reasonably good relationship with them. The Jew Abraham of Berkhampstead had been imprisoned in 1254 on suspicion of murdering his wife. More than this, Matthew Paris recounts, the murder had been preceded by a grotesque scene in which Abraham was alleged to have taken an image of the Virgin Mary with Christ on her lap and defecated on it in his latrine. Abraham killed his wife, Paris says, because she had presumed to clean the image.[28] However unlikely this extraordinary tale was, Abraham was released only on payment of a large sum to the king and declared to be the personal property of Richard of Cornwall, who was also the lord of Berkhampstead. The debts owing to Abraham were worth some £1,800, but they were to be collected and used by Richard himself.[29] Even more heavily involved in the Jewish debt trade was the queen, Eleanor of Provence. English queens were entitled to 'queen's gold', a levy of 10 per cent on voluntary payments to the king of ten marks or more. The definition of 'voluntary payment' was broad, however. In this way, the queen received gold on the third part of a deceased Jew's property, and she even received 10 per cent on the £40,000 tallage of 1244. As has been shown in the latest study of Eleanor of Provence, she was often prepared to take payment in the form of Jewish bonds. This would allow her to take control of the property which had been used as security for the loan. Thus Eleanor acquired the lands of William de Lascelles which were worth £20 a year. These were the security for a debt which William had entered into with Aaron of York in 1257.[30] As will be seen, she continued to be heavily involved with Jewish finance well into the reign of her son, Edward I. Such conduct on behalf of members of the king's family and his ministers only served to stir up further resentment towards the Jews and jealousy towards those great men and women who were able to take advantage of the financial difficulties of others. Amongst the grievances of those barons who sought to reform the government of the kingdom in 1258 was one which addressed precisely these concerns. The complaint was that Jews often transferred their debts 'to magnates and other persons powerful in the kingdom… and although those who owe the debt are ready to pay it, with the interest, the magnates put off the matter, in order that by hook or by crook the lands and holdings shall remain in their hands'.[31] The desperate cry of the small landholder under financial pressure can be heard loud and clear in this clause of the Petition of the Barons.

Indeed, it is the financial plight of such men which has prompted some historians to speak in terms of a general 'crisis of the knightly class' in thirteenth-century England. One, indeed, has observed that, in the 1200s, 'Jewish moneylending was a symptom of a general economic crisis'.[32] The number of knights in England certainly declined as the thirteenth century went on. The reasons for this are complex and varied. However, by 1200, being a knight meant much more than sitting armed on a horse. Knights were the backbone of local political society and were required to staff juries, commissions and other local offices. Because they were given such responsibilities by the king and his officials, the view developed that only men deemed fit to take on the burden of knighthood should be allowed the status conferred by the title. In other words, a knight should be a man who could afford the right equipment and support an adequate retinue. Not surprisingly, therefore, only the better off could afford to maintain their claims to knightly rank. Many less affluent knights appear simply to have abandoned their titles and settled for a cheaper life without military and administrative responsibilities. Others, however, in the drive to keep up appearances, were plunged into debt. And this is where the Jews entered the picture. Men might sell land or possessions to a richer neighbour or a religious house; just as often, however, they may have tried to defray the costs of knighthood by borrowing from a Jewish lender. There were certainly many knightly clients (as well as debtors from other social groups) on the books of a great Jewish financier like Aaron le Blund of Hereford by the 1270s, and examples abound from other parts of the country, too. The case of Stephen de Chenduit has already been mentioned.[33] And in northern England the local gentry was prepared to involve itself with Jewish credit on an extensive scale. Indeed, it has been claimed that, by the mid-thirteenth century, it would be 'safe to conclude that a large proportion of the northern "knightly class" were not only borrowing from York Jews but were also finding it difficult to extricate themselves from their entanglements'. The average size of those Yorkshire debts which are known about was about £50 or £60, but some were much larger.[34] Despite such evidence, however, it is difficult to argue that levels of debt were insupportable for large numbers of English knights by the mid-thirteenth century. It is equally difficult confidently to support the view that knightly indebtedness to the Jews led to 'one of the most significant economic movements of thirteenth-century England, a large scale shift of landed wealth from all kinds of "declining" families towards the newly rich'.[35] Nevertheless, there is no doubt that better-off Christians and religious houses profited from the difficulties of their more needy brethren during the thirteenth century, and that lands used as security for Jewish loans were acquired by opportunistic entrepreneurs and speculators. The consequence of such developments for the politicians of the 1250s and 1260s may have been that a ready-made constituency of disgruntled lesser landholders, which included men like Stephen de Chenduit, was ready to listen to the leader who offered them a way out of their difficulties.

England's Jews were thus caught in an impossible situation in the two decades either side of 1250. They needed to keep raising large sums of money if they were to maintain their relationship with the king and carry on trading at all. In doing this, however, they impoverished themselves and many of their Christian clients. Thus as royal financial pressure on the

Jews increased, so did the anger and hatred directed towards them. There were several high-profile Jewish casualties during these years. Aaron of York's descent into poverty has already been mentioned. Another whose career was ruined was Elias l'Eveske. In the 1230s, he was one of the leading members of London's Jewish community, and in 1243 he was appointed archpresbyter by Henry III. Elias therefore had the thankless task of steering England's Jews through the turbulent waters of the 1240s and early 1250s. But he did not help himself when he ensured that he and his family were granted exemptions from royal tax demands. He became increasingly unpopular with his co-religionists and finally, in 1257, he was removed from office after being accused of continuing to collect payment of debts which he had previously transferred to Richard of Cornwall. Then Hagin and Cresse, sons of Master Moses of London, paid the king three gold marks to make sure that Elias was never restored to his office, and to be allowed to elect their own archpresbyter. Hagin succeeded Elias as archpresbyter in 1258. More scandal ensued late in the same year, however, when one of Elias's servants was alleged to have been responsible for a vicious attack on Hagin. Elias and his two sons managed to bring an end to the prosecution only by converting to Christianity in January 1259. Their property, valued at £2,666, was confiscated by the king and sold to another Elias, the brother of Hagin and Cresse.[36]

The 1250s also saw yet another of those periodic bursts of crusading enthusiasm and of heightened anti-Jewish feeling on the European mainland. In 1253–4, for example, whilst he was in the Holy Land, King Louis IX of France issued another set of restrictive measures aimed at limiting Jewish lending and religious practice within his lands in France. Jews were ordered to desist from usury, blasphemy, magic and necromancy; copies of the Talmud were to be burned; and, almost as if to give a foretaste of the provisions of Edward I's Statute of Jewry of

1275, all Jews were ordered to live by manual labour or by non-usurious trade. Any Jew who was unwilling to abide by these rules was to be expelled from the royal lands, and it seems that this was not an empty threat.[37] England was never likely to remain insulated from such developments. In his Statute of Jewry issued in January 1253, Henry III ordered that 'no Jew remain in England unless he do the King service, and that from the hour of birth every Jew, whether male or female, serve Us in some way'. The statute went on to order, amongst other things, that no new synagogues were to be built in England; services in existing synagogues were to be conducted quietly, 'that Christians may not hear them'; male Jews were not to have Christian nurses and no Jew was to have Christian servants; they were not to have sexual relations with Christians; and they were henceforth to reside only in towns with established Jewish communities. Also, the wearing of the tabula was to be more strictly enforced: every Jew was to 'wear his badge conspicuously on his breast'.[38] It is probably right to say that 'the year 1253 was a major turning point in the constitutional status of the Jew'.[39] And given their difficulties, it is hardly surprising that, in 1255, England's Jews, at this time still led by Elias l'Eveske, made a desperate plea for royal permission to leave the kingdom. They had not outlived their financial usefulness to the crown just yet, however, and permission was refused.[40]

Anti-Jewish feeling manifested itself in other ways in the 1250s. Matthew Paris's incredible description of the story of Abraham of Berkhampstead has already been recounted; but it was the recurrence of the blood libel which did the greatest damage to the Jews' reputation. Since the case of William of Norwich in 1144, the ritual murder accusation against the Jews had developed to the extent that it was now commonly believed that they annually crucified a Christian boy as a sacrifice and to insult Christ. In the thirteenth century, such allegations continued to be made: at Lincoln in 1202, for example,

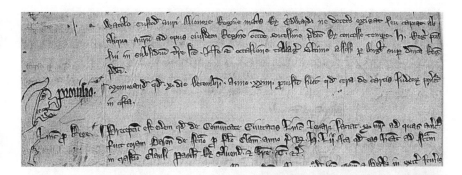

Above: 1 Portrait of a Jew, 1271–2. This caricature portrait of a Jew, included in the margin of a roll containing copies of royal writs and orders, shows him hooded with an exaggeratedly long hook-nose and a beard. The word 'Provisio' comes out of the image's mouth in order to draw attention to the order in question, which stipulated that the wax used for the sealing of Jewish charters was to be placed in a chest. The order itself dated from December 1239; it is not clear why it appears in a roll from 1271–2.

Right: 2 Portrait of a Jew, 1277. Caricature portrait of a Jew, Aaron 'son of the Devil', included in the margin of a roll of pleas of the Forest, against a case concerning the killing of a doe at Colchester in Essex by Jews and Christians. Two of the accused in the case were Aaron's son Cok (Isaac) and Samuel. The drawing shows Aaron wearing the tabula, the piece of cloth cut to resemble the supposed shape of the stone tablets which bore the Ten Commandments.

Above left: 3 Jews in the Book of Genesis. Here three episodes from the Book of Genesis are illustrated in the so-called Great Lambeth Bible, probably produced at Canterbury in about 1150. The first, in the top compartment, shows Abraham entertaining the angels (chap. 18). The second, the sacrifice of Isaac (chap. 22), is on the right of the panel below. Abraham, wearing the distinctive rounded Jewish cap with a knob on the top, is about to strike Isaac with his sword, only to be fended off by an angel. The greater part of the panel, however, is taken up with a depiction of Jacob's dream of the ladder (chap. 28). Jacob, shown both asleep and awake, is also wearing the rounded cap.

Above right: 4 Jews in the Book of Numbers. On this folio of the Great Lambeth Bible, several scenes from the Book of Numbers are depicted. On the right of the top compartment, Moses is seen on Mount Sinai (1:1), whilst on the left he is counting out the tribes of Israel (1:2). In the bottom compartment are represented the duties of the Levites in the tending of the tabernacle (chaps 3 and 4). These depictions are again interesting for their obvious use of the conventional Jewish headgear, the rounded cap with a knob.

Opposite above: 5 Jews in the Book of Ruth. On this folio of the Great Lambeth Bible, several scenes from the Book of Ruth are depicted. On the left, Ruth is shown gleaning in the fields whilst Boaz, holding a scroll and wearing the rounded Jewish cap, looks on (chap. 2). In the centre she appears before Naomi with what she has gleaned (2:18) and on the right she appears at the feet of a bareheaded Boaz (3:7–9).

agrum booz ad colligendas spicas.
in Booz dar licenciam ruth uc de agro ei colligam spi
cas & hora uescendi cu messoribus comedar pco

ten filie syon. Explic
prologus.
Incipit liber ruth.

Right: 6 The Flight into Egypt (St Albans Psalter, English, *c.*1123). Here, the Holy Family, led by Joseph's son James, is shown fleeing Herod's soldiers after the birth of Christ (Matthew 2:14). Joseph is depicted wearing a version of the conventional Jewish headgear, the rounded Jewish cap with a knob on top.

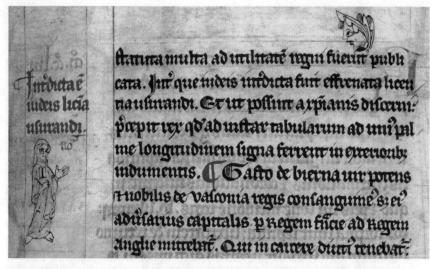

7 Sketch of a Jew (*Chronica Roffense*, English, early fourteenth century). This sketch of a Jew, in the margin of an English chronicle of the early 1300s, against an account of the Statute of Jewry of 1275 and an order to wear the tabula, shows him wearing the latter, the pieces of cloth cut to resemble the supposed shape of the stone tablets which bore the Ten Commandments. Above the Jew's head in red is the statement 'Jews are forbidden to take part in usury'.

8 Portraits of Several Jews, 1233. This famous and extraordinary image is found at the head of an Exchequer roll of 1233 recording receipts from a Jewish tallage. Amongst other things, it includes a depiction of Isaac of Norwich, one of the wealthiest Jewish financiers of the period, with three faces. It also shows two of his associates, Mosse Mokke (wearing the distinctive Jewish headgear, the pointed *pileum cornutum*) and Abigail (or Avegay), apparently being tortured by devils. The precise meaning or purpose of the illustration is unclear.

Jews were suspected of killing a child whose body was found outside the city walls; and at London in 1244 marks inscribed on the arms, legs and chest of a dead child found in St Benedict's cemetery were thought to be Hebrew words.[41] However, the most notorious case of the thirteenth century was that of Hugh of Lincoln (known as 'Little St Hugh' to distinguish him from St Hugh, who had been bishop of Lincoln at the end of the twelfth century), for whose death in 1255 nineteen Jews were executed.[42] There are several accounts of what happened to Hugh, but the one which has received most attention was written by Matthew Paris, according to whom Hugh disappeared, kidnapped by Jews, on about 29 June 1255. He was then kept alive for ten days, Paris recounted, during which time Jews from across England were summoned to take part in his torture and murder. They enacted a parody of the crucifixion by stabbing Hugh with knives; they then stabbed him through the heart and disembowelled him. Attempts to bury Hugh's body failed, however, as the earth refused to receive the desecrated corpse, and so it was thrown down a well outside the house of a prominent local Jew, Copin. Then, on hearing that her son had last been seen entering Copin's house, Hugh's mother discovered the body in the well and summoned the bailiffs. Copin then confessed to the crime on being offered immunity from prosecution. However, when Henry III himself arrived in Lincoln and heard what had happened, Copin was taken, drawn and hanged. Other Jews were seized and taken to London. Another account of this episode was compiled at Burton Abbey. According to this, Hugh disappeared on 31 July 1255, having been kidnapped by Jopin [*sic*], the leader of Lincoln's Jews. He was then starved for twenty-six days. Meanwhile, other Jews were summoned and, when they arrived, the boy was mutilated and then crucified on 27 August. Hugh's mother made her enquiries and suspicions were raised by the presence of an unusually large number of Jews in the city. They explained that they were there to celebrate a wedding. This story counted for little, however, when Hugh's body was discovered in a well on 29 August. The king arrived in Lincoln a month or so later, when he ordered an investigation and the arrest of the Jews. Ninety-one were imprisoned; Copin was executed immediately and a further eighteen later suffered the same fate. Before this, however, all accounts agree that Hugh's body had already been taken in solemn procession by the canons of Lincoln to the cathedral where he was buried and commemorated as a martyr. The cult of Little St Hugh was soon established, and the income of the cathedral chapter was bound to increase as a result. Here, in fact, may lie the key to the story. Copin's confession was central to the case against Hugh's alleged murderers, but it seems to have been extracted from him by a veteran royal servant, John of Lexinton. It is surely no coincidence that John's brother was Henry of Lexinton, the recently elected bishop of Lincoln.[43]

There are problems with all the versions of this sensational story, and the truth behind it is now lost. It may be that those Jews who were in Lincoln for a society wedding in the summer of 1255 were simply in the wrong place at the wrong time. A young boy died in unexplained circumstances; perhaps he fell down a well accidentally and drowned. On the discovery of his body, however, it was easy to blame the Jews and Copin's 'confession' seemed to confirm their guilt. In one sense, the tale of St Hugh is little different in its essentials from other ritual murder stories of the twelfth and thirteenth centuries. What sets it apart, however, and what gave it lasting power, was the stamp of royal approval given to it by Henry III. For the first time, the blood libel had been sanctioned by the government, and this could only imperil the Jews further. It is certainly right to say that, taken together, 'the corrosive effects of excessive tallages on the one side and of increased anti-Jewish propaganda and blood-libel accusations on the other seem to have made the mid-1250s a real watershed in the history of Anglo-Jewish relations'.[44]

The Jews were not the only focus for hostility in England during the 1250s, however. Henry III's government was unpopular and resentment towards it was coming to a head.[45] There were tensions at court generated by the rivalry between Queen Eleanor's uncles from Savoy and the king's half-brothers, the sons of his mother's second marriage to a great noble from Poitou in southern France, Hugh de Lusignan. Henry's reputation had also suffered, as his foreign policy had descended into something approaching farce. The king's campaign in Poitou in 1242 (towards which the Jews had contributed heavily) had ended in embarrassing withdrawal and had dealt a conclusive blow to any hope of recovering the lands lost to the French king in 1204. And even though Henry had acquitted himself better in Gascony in 1253, his expensive plans to install his second son, Edmund, as king of Sicily only served to reinforce the view that the English king was a simple man with no strategic vision or martial ability. But unhappiness with Henry's government was also felt well below the highest levels of political society. In order to raise money for his campaigns and schemes, Henry's agents bore down heavily on those with any ability to pay. It has already been seen how royal pressure on the Jews to meet their tallage obligations led in turn to pressure being placed on their Christian debtors to pay off their loans. To be sure, the Jews were resented because of this; but the government did not escape criticism. More generally, the king's relatives and courtiers were despised, as has been seen, because of the way they acquired Jewish debts and, in due course, the lands on which they were secured. But the king's local officials, particularly his sheriffs, were also widely viewed as corrupt and oppressive. Such sentiments allowed the perception to develop that magnates close to the king were abusing their local power without any possibility of being held to account in the courts, and that the king was ignoring the interests of his subjects in his desire to retain the support of his grasping favourites. The fact that many of the latter were foreigners did not tend to make disgruntled native Englishmen feel any happier about the influence they wielded. Matters first reached boiling point at a great parliament held at Westminster in the spring of 1258. The opponents of the regime, all with their own grievances against the king and his favourites, came into the open and forced Henry to agree to a reform of the realm. Seven years of political revolution and civil war had begun, and England's Jews were to be caught in the eye of the political storm.

Between 1258 and 1261, King Henry III was reduced to a figurehead as real political power in England was exercised by a council of barons. The council was to choose the king's ministers and supervise central government generally. It set out to address the grievances which had made Henry's own rule so unpopular. However, early in 1261 its power collapsed and the king was able to regain and hold control until the spring of 1263. At this point, leadership of the reform movement was assumed by the earl of Leicester, Simon de Montfort, and his dynamism and skill enabled him to wrest control of the government from the king once more. The climax of this phase of the conflict came at Lewes on 14 May 1264, when Montfort won a crushing victory over the royalists and captured the king, his brother Richard and the king's eldest son, Edward. By this time, however, England's Jews, and those in London in particular, had already suffered at the hands of the mob and of Montfort's supporters. The tone had first been set at the end of 1262. Some time shortly after 11 November, the London Jewry was attacked following an incident in which a Christian was alleged to have been stabbed by a Jew in Colechurch Lane. Many Jewish houses were destroyed and their goods were seized. If the mayor and sheriffs of the city had not intervened to stop the violence, it might have escalated further.[46] But worse was to follow in 1264. On about 7 April the London Jewry was attacked again. According to one account, Montfort was at Northampton when news reached him of a

Jewish plot. He returned quickly to London, which, vitally in the context of the civil war, his supporters controlled, where he was told that the Jews were planning to burn down the city. They had forged keys to all the city gates, it was alleged, and they had dug tunnels connecting all of the gates together. Montfort's men exacted their punishment and many of the London Jews were killed. Only those who were prepared to give information, or those who were prepared to convert, were spared.[47] The same story as told by Thomas Wykes ascribed the conduct of the attackers to greed; warfare was an expensive business after all. Neither young nor old were spared, unless they could pay for the privilege or unless they agreed to convert, and the 'most illustrious' Jew of the city, Cok, son of Abraham, was killed by John FitzJohn, one of Montfort's more important supporters, with his bare hands.[48] There are no truly reliable estimates of how many Jews died in the attack of April 1264, but the sources suggest that at least 400 and perhaps more than 500 were killed. The survivors took refuge with their *archa*, again with the help of the mayor and the sheriffs, in the Tower.[49] If these figures represent anything like the reality, the London Jewry must have been wiped out almost entirely. A London chronicler put it starkly: 'in the week before Palm Sunday [1264], the Jewry in London was destroyed'.[50] And the violence was not confined to London alone. The Dunstable annalist, after describing what had happened in the city, ominously remarked that Gilbert de Clare, Earl of Gloucester 'did the same to the Jews of Canterbury'. And there were other anti-Jewish attacks at Worcester, Lincoln, Bedford, Bristol, Northampton and Kingston.[51]

Such savagery, unknown on this scale in England since 1189–90, requires some explanation. As well as being a superb soldier and a brilliant politician, Montfort was a religious zealot. It has already been seen how he expelled the Jews from Leicester in the early 1230s in order to enhance his own claims to religious orthodoxy and to consolidate local support. He also did this,

however, because, in the words of one great historian of the
thirteenth century, Montfort 'hated Jews'.[52] Then later, in the
1260s, with the political situation so finely balanced, Montfort
could not afford to lose the backing of the citizens of London
which he had enjoyed since his supporters had come to power
there in 1263. Therefore, if the persecution of London's Jews
appeased his followers, many of whom were themselves probably in debt to Jewish lenders, and if it supplemented their
funds and his own as Wykes alleged it did, it was unlikely that
he would seek to prevent the outrage. In the aftermath of the
attacks, Montfort cancelled the debts owed by his supporters
to the Jews.[53] But the attacks of 1264 were motivated by more
than financial anxieties alone. After all, levels of indebtedness to
the Jews had probably been higher in the 1230s than they were
in the 1260s, and the earlier period had not witnessed anything
as ferocious as the anti-Jewish violence of the later one. What
was new in the 1260s, however, was the fear that indebtedness
'would lead to the permanent loss of the land on which these
debts were secured'.[54] This had not been such a concern in the
1230s for two reasons: Jews themselves were only allowed to
keep control of forfeited property for as long as it took to pay
off what they were owed; and before the early 1240s, Jewish
lenders were financially secure enough to be patient with their
demands. This all changed after 1241 as the government bore
down on the finances of its Jewish subjects and forced them to
sell off their debts 'short' to Christians whose primary interest
was probably the secured property rather than the recovery of
the loan. What was also important, however, was that 'this period
between 1263 and 1265 saw the apotheosis of all the xenophobia
that had been gathering force during Henry's reign'.[55] This had
first been directed primarily at the foreign relatives of the king
and queen, but Montfort had built his case for seizing power on
the argument that he was keeping England for the English and
protecting the interests of the native 'community of the realm'.

Montfort's own French origins did not appear to dampen his enthusiasm for keeping aliens out of office in England, and 'more than anything else the issue unified his movement and gave it meaning, so much so that chroniclers came to see the oppression by foreigners as the sole cause of the revolution of 1258'.[56] This rising tide of xenophobia reached its hysterical peak at a time when, as has been seen, specifically anti-Jewish feeling was particularly intense. And whilst there is no easy correlation between those men who supported Montfort and those who were indebted to Jews, the latter were still identified in the popular imagination as representatives of the oppressive financial arm of an unpopular government as well as the killers of innocent Christian children. In England during the mid-1260s, the Jews would have had more reason than most other 'aliens' to fear for their safety.

And the persecution continued beyond 1264, despite attempts by the government to deal with it. After his victory at Lewes in May of that year, Simon de Montfort controlled England for nearly fifteen months; Henry III was reduced to a cipher. During this period, Montfort's administration issued orders in the king's name, to the authorities in London and Winchester in June 1264 for example, that the Jews in those cities should be protected and allowed to return peacefully to their homes. And in May 1265, an order was issued which attempted to protect the Jews of Lincoln from attack, because 'certain persons threaten mischief against them'.[57] Such orders, however, did not prevent Montfort's own son, also called Simon, destroying the Winchester Jewry when he seized and plundered the city in July 1265.[58] And even after Earl Simon himself had been defeated and killed at the battle of Evesham in August 1265, the Jews remained exposed. In the aftermath of the royalist victory, rebel lands were seized and redistributed by the king to his supporters. Many of Montfort's erstwhile followers therefore, the so-called 'Disinherited', faced ruin and had little to lose by continuing to oppose the king. Several centres of resistance were established, at Montfort's castle of Kenilworth, for example, and another on the Isle of Axholme in Lincolnshire. Amongst those who went to Axholme was the knight John de Deyville.[59] He was also part of a rebel army which was defeated at Chesterfield by a royalist force in May 1266, after which defeat Deyville proceeded to sack Lincoln. In the process he singled out the Lincoln Jews and killed many of them. He also desecrated the synagogue and burnt as many Jewish bonds and charters as he could find.[60] Deyville was heavily in debt to Jewish lenders, so it is no surprise that he and his followers acted in this way. And this was not an isolated phenomenon by any means. *Archae* were destroyed or removed in many towns during the civil war. In the end, though, most debtors probably did not benefit from the disruption. In 1266–7, for example, the newly restored royal administration made grants to the Jews of Bristol and Bedford, and to Aaron, the son of Leo le Blund of London, which would have reassured the lenders: although their *archae* had been destroyed in the war, the debts remained recoverable if reasonable proof of them was still available.[61] Such measures were implemented at roughly the same time that Henry III reversed Montfort's decision to relieve Jewish debtors of their obligations to their creditors. The debts were still payable, the king said, as he tried to get the Jewish community back on its feet.[62]

Another royal concession to the Jews was granted in May 1269, albeit at a price. In return for a payment of £1,000, the Jews were to be freed from the payment of tallage for three years, unless, that is, the king or his son Edward went on crusade during that period, in which case a tallage could be levied.[63] This is in effect what happened. In August 1270, Edward left England for the Holy Land, having taken the cross at Northampton in June 1268. He had remained at home during the intervening two years whilst men and resources were gathered together for his expedition. Edward was certainly in great need of funds,

and as part of the money-raising effort Henry III granted his
son £4,000 from the English Jewry, a third of which was to
be provided by Richard of Cornwall, who in turn was granted
the Jewry for a year so as to recover his debt.[64] Thus, whilst
apparently keen to help the Jews recover after the civil war, the
king was still prepared to press them hard when he thought
it necessary to do so. In April 1269, for example, the sheriffs
of Oxfordshire and Berkshire were ordered to clamp down
on Jews in their jurisdictions found living outside towns with
recognised Jewish communities or *archae*.[65] And nowhere was
the tightness of this royal hold over the Jews better expressed
than in the so-called 'Provisions of the Jewry' of 1269. These
new regulations were drafted during the course of a parliament
held in January 1269, and they were made public in April of the
same year.[66] They are not easy to interpret; they were 'drafted
with such ambiguous brevity that the precise limitations meant
to be imposed are in doubt'.[67] They were expressly designed,
however, 'for the better ordering of the land and the relief of
the Christians from the burdens laid upon them by the Jewry
of England'. In other words, the provisions were intended to
restrict Jewish moneylending activities. More particularly they
were aimed at bringing an end to the practice whereby Jewish
lenders lent money to Christians in return for the creation of
annual rent-charges on the Christians' lands. Such activity had
become increasingly common, it seems, during the second half
of the thirteenth century; but more worrying for the debtor
was the fear that the debt might be acquired by a third party,
usually a Christian and often a high-ranking minister or relation
of the king. As has been seen, if the debt went unpaid, the result
was often the loss of the land itself.[68] The ordinance stipulated
that all such transactions should be prohibited in the future, all
existing ones should be cancelled if they had not already been
transferred to a third party, and that none should be sold on to
a third party in the future. More generally, it was provided that

henceforth no debt of any kind could be sold by a Jew without
royal permission; and if such a debt was sold legitimately to
a Christian, the purchaser would take it on without interest.
Clearly, the purpose of this ordinance was to assist those who
were suffering at the hands of Jewish lenders and their Christian
associates. It will be suggested in the next chapter what the Lord
Edward, who was expressly identified with the making of the
provisions in their preamble, received in return for his efforts on
behalf of these indebted lesser landholders.[69] For Jewish lenders, however, the implications of the new rules must have been
deeply troubling. Their scope for lending had been reduced and
many of the great men of the kingdom, those who had profited
from the trafficking in these debts before 1269, now had less
reason than ever to wish for the continued maintenance of a
Jewish presence in England.

Further severe restrictions were placed on the operation
of Jewish commercial life in July 1271, when the king in the
so-called *Provisio Judaismi* ordered that Jews were henceforth
forbidden to acquire a freehold 'in manors, lands, tenements,
fees, rents or tenures of any kind whatsoever'.[70] Put bluntly, Jews
were prohibited from holding any land except the houses they
already occupied or owned. Once again the purpose of this
enactment was to restrict the Jews' opportunities for lending
on the security of land; if they could not hold land themselves
(hitherto they had been allowed to do so until the particular debt had been paid off), there was no point contracting
a loan secured on it. Other forms of security could still be
used, commodities and possessions for example, but these would
have tended to be less valuable and therefore less attractive to
the lender. Again it is impossible to be sure how strictly this
order was enforced in the years following its issue. However,
the sentiments it expressed are in some ways just as important
as its practical effects. Taken together, the regulations of 1269
and 1271 signalled the beginning of a royal campaign against

Jewish lending which was to go on for the next twenty years. This campaign went through various stages, as will be seen, and it was by no means consistent or predictable in its course. Nevertheless, the tide had turned by 1272. On 25 November of that year, a London Jew called Benedict son of Cok was 'in hiding in the Tower of London because of the king's death' nine days earlier. Then at some time in the following year, the Jews of Nottingham gave the new king four gold bezants for a writ ordering the sheriff to 'see that they be so treated as in the time of King Henry'.[71] Doubtless Benedict had his own reasons for taking refuge as he did; nor is it clear precisely what fears the Jewish community in Nottingham might have had at this time. But such examples may be seen as expressing the uncertainty probably felt by many English Jews as Henry III's reign came to an end. It had begun promisingly and with the hope on the Jews' part that they would be able to put the difficulties of John's reign behind them. However, as Henry grew to maturity and as his religious views hardened, such hopes had been disappointed. By 1272, English Jewry was on the brink of ruin. It was not alone in this; across the Channel the reign of Louis IX, which had been almost as long as Henry III's in England, 'had been an unmitigated disaster' for the Jews of northern France.[72] That their French co-religionists had arguably suffered even worse than they had was probably no comfort to England's Jews, however. For them, it was unclear what the future held in 1272, and there was little reason for them to think that things could only get better.

5

King Edward I
and the Jews

No English king of the Middle Ages is more closely associated with the Jews than Edward I (1272–1307). This is hardly surprising. It was Edward who ruled during the final years of England's medieval Jewry; thus the entire history of the Jews in England after 1066 culminates in the momentous events of his reign. It is important, therefore, to try and get some idea of what Edward thought about the Jews and how his views developed over time. After all, if it was Edward who ultimately took the decision to expel the Jews from the kingdom in 1290, little meaningful sense can be made of this event without some effort to understand the motivation of the man behind it. Given the nature of the available evidence, this is not easy. As will be seen, the Expulsion came about for a variety of reasons, some short-term, some long-term, some political, some financial, some religious and some personal to the king himself. However, there was

nothing inevitable about the events of 1290 and serious efforts
to deal with the Jews in other ways were tried before they
were ordered to leave England. It is in these events and in
the circumstances surrounding them that the causes of the
Expulsion remain to be uncovered.

The future Edward I (or 'the Lord Edward' as he was known
before he became king) was born at Westminster in June 1239.
His genuinely pious father, Henry III, had named his eldest son
after Edward the Confessor, to whose cult Henry was devoted.
Edward himself does not really emerge from the records until
1254, when his marriage to a Spanish princess, Eleanor of
Castile, was arranged. Eleanor's half-brother, Alfonso X of
Castile, was keen to ensure that Edward should bring a substantial landed endowment into the marriage with him, and so
Henry III granted the young prince Gascony, Ireland, the earl-
dom of Chester and extensive estates in Wales and England.[1]
At the beginning of that period of political crisis in England
which lasted from 1258 until 1265, Edward allied himself with
the Lusignans, the king's unpopular half-brothers from Poitou;
but in 1259 he joined those seeking to reform the government
of the kingdom and fell from his father's favour as a result. By
1262, however, Henry and Edward had been reconciled, and
it was in that year that Edward appears to have had his first
meaningful contact with the English Jewry. In June 1262 the
Jewry was granted to Edward for three years by the king. This
was hardly a generous gesture by Henry, however, and was
more a consequence of royal displeasure. The lands Edward had
been granted at the time of his marriage had been misman-
aged, and Henry III seems to have thought that Edward and
his ministers could not be trusted with them any longer. So in
return for the grant of the Jewry, Edward was obliged to surrender to Henry III significant parts of what he had been given
in 1254. The funds from the Jewry were supposed to plug the
gap in Edward's finances caused by this surrender. However,

the Jewry clearly did not provide Edward with funds quickly
enough, and in mid-1263 he transferred it to some Cahorsin
merchants.[2] It is not clear what he got in return, but it is likely
to have been a considerable sum.

By this time, Edward was firmly in the royalist camp, and
staunchly opposed to his uncle Simon de Montfort (Montfort
was married to Henry III's sister, Eleanor). Edward was captured along with his father when Montfort triumphed at the
battle of Lewes in May 1264 and he remained imprisoned until
March 1265. At that point, officially at least, he was released;
but this was something of a sham and Edward remained in
effect in captivity until he escaped in May. He then won a great
victory for the royalists at Evesham in August 1265 and led the
campaign which dealt with the remnants of the rebel cause
thereafter. It was at the end of this phase of Edward's life that
one incident occurred which may have affected his attitude to
the Jews.[3] In Oxford on Ascension Day (17 May) in 1268, it
was alleged that some members of the Jewish community there
'snatched a portable cross, carried about in solemn procession
on the said day, from the hands of its bearer, outrageously
broke it and prostrated it on the ground in contempt'. The
procession was attacked whilst walking down St Aldates, where
Christ Church now stands, which at this time was the heart
of the Oxford Jewry. The attack, therefore, was not random or
senseless; more likely, it was intended to show how angry the
Jews were about an ostentatious Christian ritual taking place
in the middle of their community. Nevertheless, this insult was
reported to Henry III and to Edward, who was in Oxford at
the time. The Oxford Jews were eventually compelled to pay
for a cross to replace the one that had been broken; but they
were also forced to pay for a fixed marble cross which was
erected threateningly near their synagogue. This incident took
place just over five weeks before the next important event in
Edward's life. In June 1268 at Northampton Edward was the

most prominent amongst a group of leading English magnates who vowed to go on crusade. The Oxford episode occurred, therefore, in the approach to yet another period of crusading enthusiasm, and presumably at a time when Edward's own religious sensibilities were more heightened than usual. Edward was certainly enthusiastic about the crusade. It would give him a chance to display his martial abilities and enable him to escape England and its problems for a while. He may have seen it as his last opportunity to give free rein to his youthful energies and passions before assuming the onerous burden of kingship. And Edward's crusading intentions certainly might have prompted him to take a keener and more personal interest in Jewish affairs. He may also have been influenced further by events in France. Three months after the incident at Oxford, in September 1268, King Louis IX ordered a general confiscation of Jewish goods and property throughout his lands. It has been suggested that this seizure formed part of Louis's own crusading preparations. It was followed by harsher royally sponsored anti-Jewish measures which made the final years of Louis's reign (he died on crusade in August 1270) extremely difficult ones for the Jews of northern France.[4]

It was against this background that the Provisions of the Jewry were issued in England in 1269. Published only a year after the outrage in Oxford, they were said to have been made by the king 'with the advice of the Lord Edward, his eldest son, and his other trusty lieges'.[5] John Maddicott has argued convincingly that the Provisions were closely linked with Edward's preparations for the crusade.[6] Crusading was an expensive business, and the best way to obtain funds was by securing a grant of a tax in parliament. This period was a formative one in the development of that institution. By the 1260s, it was accepted by the king and his subjects alike that general taxation needed the consent at least of the baronage. However, it was also acknowledged that it was sensible to secure consent to taxation from as wide

a section of the political community as possible. This meant
that knights from the shires and burgesses from the towns were
being included more often in taxation negotiations. In 1254 two
knights from each shire had been summoned to London to consider Henry III's request for a tax, for example, and in 1268 the
royal government began a new campaign to secure the consent
of the magnates and the commons to a tax for the crusade. At
a parliament held in July 1269, a tax of a twentieth of the value
of moveable goods was granted in principle to the king for the
purposes of the crusade, although it was not finally confirmed
until April 1270. The negotiations which led to the grant of this
tax were long and complex; the final concession allowed by the
king in order to secure the tax was his confirmation of Magna
Carta and the Charter of the Forest. However, the issue of the
Provisions of the Jewry should be seen in this context, too. It
was at a parliament held in January 1269 that the Provisions
were drafted, and they were published at another parliament in
April of the same year. Their purpose was 'to offer relief to small
landowners, gentry, knights and minor barons, at the expense
both of the Jews and of the magnates who had profited from
the difficulties of their inferiors'.[7] Many of these men, of course,
had suffered financially during the recent civil war, and, if they
had not fallen into debt before the war, many former rebels
became indebted to the Jews as a result of having to pay fines
to recover their confiscated lands after it. The Provisions were
therefore a bid for their support, and it is no surprise that the
Lord Edward wished to be personally associated with them. It
is surely no coincidence that, on 14 May 1270, only just over
two weeks after the final grant of the twentieth for the crusade,
the king ordered that the 1269 Provisions were to be enforced.[8]
This 'should almost certainly be seen as a concession made by
Henry in the process of gaining consent to the collection of the
tax from the parliamentary knights who represented the smaller
landholders of the shires'.[9]

It would be misleading to describe the Provisions of the Jewry as anything other than an anti-Jewish measure. Designed as they were to restrict Jewish trading activity, they must have had a serious impact on the affairs and finances of the Jewish community. However, this was not their primary objective. Edward backed the provisions, not because of what they would do to the Jews, but because they would help those Christians whose political and financial support he needed. At this stage, however, Jewish issues must have come into focus for Edward only briefly. He left England in August 1270, and even the death of his father Henry III in November 1272 did not bring him home quickly. He did not set foot on English soil again until 2 August 1274, when he landed at Dover. During his crusade, Edward had spent time in France, Italy, Sicily and Cyprus, as well as the Holy Land itself. In that time he would almost certainly have encountered Jews and perhaps have had discussions with other European leaders about the Jews in their lands. He may even have had time to take in the renewed strictures against usury issued by the Council of Lyons in 1274. Whether the new king returned to England burning with a desire to deal with 'the Jewish problem' in England, however, is another matter. In January 1275, Edward granted his mother, Eleanor of Provence, the right to expel all Jews from the towns on her dower lands, but this probably reveals more about Queen Eleanor than it does about King Edward.[10]

Edward's agenda was a full one in 1274, and the year in government following his assumption of direct control was very active.[11] By March 1275, the Hundred Rolls inquest had been launched and carried out. Its purpose had been to inquire into lost royal rights and the oppressions of local government across the kingdom. Then, in April 1275, the first parliament of the reign was held at Westminster. Here the findings of the Hundred Rolls inquest were dealt with in the first Statute of Westminster, and a new long-term source of revenue was made available to the king when he was granted customs duties on wool exports. Perhaps Edward derived a new sense of financial stability from the customs arrangements. But he was still keen to secure the grant of a tax, and he achieved this at the second parliament of the reign, which met at Westminster in October 1275. As in 1269, this grant of direct taxation was surely not unconnected with the further consideration of Jewish lending during this parliament.[12] The resulting Statute of the Jewry has recently been described as 'the most wide-ranging, the most detailed and the most radical of all the legislation of the thirteenth century concerned with the Jewish community'.[13] And certainly, the breadth of its ambition is striking. The statute was not designed to destroy or incapacitate the Jewish community in England, but it was designed to point it in a new direction, away from usury and towards legitimate trade.[14] Henceforth, the statute proclaimed, 'no Jew shall lend anything at usury, either on land or rent or anything else'. It went on to state that, in respect of existing loans, no interest was to accumulate after 13 October 1275. Put simply, Jews were prohibited from lending money at interest or, indeed, where anything more than the sum loaned was to be repaid to the creditor. Such practices were now illegal. Also, there would be no more royal assistance in recovering usurious loans, and, if any Jew continued to lend at interest, the king reserved the right to 'punish him at his discretion'. The statute also contained further restrictions on the ways Jews could operate. From now on, only half of the lands and chattels of a Christian debtor would be confiscated in order to enforce payment of a debt, where previously all of the lands and chattels had been liable to confiscation; repayment could not be demanded of the heirs of a debtor unless a court had authorised such action; and no land could be handed over to the lender until it had been officially valued. The statute also stipulated that no Jew could make a permanent grant of any house, rent or tenement he owned without royal permission; nor could he acquit any Christian of a debt without the king's consent. Other parts of the statute were more conventional and echoed the provisions of earlier Jewish legislation. All Jews were to live in towns with an *archa*, it said, and there was an attempt more rigorously to enforce previous pronouncements about the physical appearance of the Jews. Every Jew from the age of seven 'shall wear a distinguishing mark on his outer garment, that is to say in the form of two Tables joined, of yellow felt of the length of six inches and of the breadth of three inches'. Furthermore, all Jews, male or female, over the age of twelve were to pay the king an annual tax at Easter of three pence.

These rules were based firmly and explicitly in the statute on the principle that each Jew was the king's 'serf' or 'bondman'. On this basis, the statute made clear, and because the Church required their preservation, the Jews would continue to receive royal protection. However, things could not continue as they had in the past. The prohibition of usury was the overriding aim of the statute; however, in the future, the statute went on, the Jews 'may live by lawful trade and by their labour'. In other words, they could become merchants instead of money-lenders, and 'they may have intercourse with Christians in order to carry on lawful trade by selling and buying'. Such provisions were not completely novel; something similar had been attempted by Louis IX in France in 1253–4.[15] However, nothing like them had been enacted before in England, and they were certainly the most radical element of the 1275 legislation. They meant that the statute was by no means a wholly negative attempt to deal with the Jewish problem. The government understood that, deprived of the ability to make money from lending, and provided with no alternative, the Jewish community in England would effectively be ruined. So Jews were to be allowed to remain peacefully in England, and the statute encouraged them to try new ways to make a living: 'on

the surface it was a well-meaning and indeed conscientious
attempt to emancipate the Jews economically'.[16] In practice,
however, matters were not as straightforward as this. Jews were
still compelled to live only in certain places; thus their ability to
trade freely and at their own discretion was seriously hampered
from the start. That they could not sell property or negotiate
debts without royal permission must also have put an obstacle
in the way of prospective Jewish traders. And then of course
the statute failed to take account of the bigotry and prejudice
of Christian society towards the Jews. After generations of
seeing Jews in a particular light, and having grown accustomed
to dealing with them in a particular capacity, it was probably
unrealistic of Edward and his advisers to think that the king's
Christian subjects were going to accept a new role for the
Jews overnight. Thus, 'the basic message of the *Statutum de
Judeismo* was that the Jew was to earn his living by competing
in Christian society like a Christian whilst at the same time
being disadvantaged by discrimination'.[17]

It is difficult to glean from the statute what Edward's own
view of his Jewish subjects was at this point in his reign. As a
loyal son of the Church he objected to usury as a sin. He also
objected to the practice, the statute claimed, 'because the king
has seen that many evils and instances of the disinheriting of
good men of his land have happened as a result of the usuries
which the Jews have made in the past'. However, Edward also
acknowledged the 'great benefit' which his predecessors had
received from the Jews. Consequently, his intention in 1275
appears to have been to strike a balance between the protection of his Jewish and Christian subjects. Inevitably, the king
is likely to have attached more weight to the concerns of the
latter than the former (after all, they had the power to grant
him taxes); but there are grounds to argue that the 1275 statute
was a thoughtful albeit flawed attempt to deal with a difficult
problem. Edward did not like the Jews and he would have

liked them all to convert to Christianity; but in 1275 he was
not already intent on eliminating them.

Whatever the extent of Edward's plans in 1275, the statute
of that year was in effect 'an attempt at radical social engineer-
ing'.[18] And the Jews of England were quick to appreciate its
implications and to view them with alarm. Shortly after the
statute was issued a petition was sent to the king by 'the commonalty of the Jews' asking for certain points regarding the
statute to be clarified or modified.[19] Amongst other things, it
asked what would happen if a debtor died without heirs and
his lands went back into the hands of his rich lord. Surely it
was unfair that the lender could still then only reclaim his
debt against half of the property. And what about those poor
Jews who could not afford to live by trade? the petition asked.
Might they have the king's permission to sell their houses to
fellow Jews? And how, the petition asked, could Jews compete
fairly with Christians in trade? Christian merchants could provide credit and expect to be paid; Jews could not. Christian
merchants 'can carry their merchandise far and near', but Jews
could not leave the *archae* towns for fear of being robbed. The
petition concluded with a request that the Jews in England
might be allowed to live as they had done under Edward's
ancestors since 1066. This was a vain request, however. Royal
policy towards the Jews would never be the same again.

For all its significance, however, and imaginative though
it was, until recently it has been generally accepted that the
'Edwardian Experiment' of 1275 was a failure. It did not
achieve its objective of bringing an end to Jewish usury, and
many Jewish lenders simply carried on as they always had done,
but in secret. For other Jews associated with lending who were
unable to do this, the prospect was bleak: conversion, crime
and starvation were the only real alternatives. Now, though,
another view has been put forward by Robin Mundill which
holds that some Jews at least did try and make the best out of

the new situation by getting involved in the trade in certain commodities, principally wool and cereals.[20] According to this theory, after 1275 Jewish merchants across England began to offer advance credit to the producers of these commodities, in return for which they would be repaid, not in cash, but with amounts of the commodities themselves which they could then sell on. Now such transactions have always been known about: the bonds recording many of them were kept in the *archae* delivered to Westminster after the Expulsion of 1290. They were not, therefore, clandestine deals. However, they have usually been regarded as purely fictitious sales which covered up conventional usurious deals – the Jews involved did not really expect to receive fleeces or sacks of corn in return for their cash. Now, however, Mundill has argued convincingly that a fair proportion of those transactions were genuine. Whether all of them were *bona fide*, however, is another matter. What is more, and given the element of profit potentially involved in even a genuine commodity transaction of this kind, it is open to question whether such a deal might have been regarded as usurious in itself and thus contrary to the terms of the 1275 statute. Nevertheless, despite these reservations, the idea that all of England's Jews were plunged into irreversible hardship and penury by the new rules of 1275 is too stark and far from certain.

Having said this, other evidence does much to show how relatively impoverished England's Jewish community had become by the 1270s. Between 1273 and 1278, no fewer than five separate tallages were imposed on the Jews.[21] One, which may have been ordered before Edward's return from crusade, but which first appears in the records in September 1274, was assessed at no less than a third of the value of all Jewish goods. Further tallages in 1276 and 1278 were assessed at £1,000 and £2,000 respectively. However, it seems that little more than £5,300 was paid in tallage by the Jews during this six-year period. This was not an inconsiderable sum in itself, of course, and it does show that there was still money in Jewish hands even after the issue of the Statute of the Jewry in 1275. However, the sums raised are negligible compared with what was being collected earlier in the century. Between 1241 and 1258, Henry III's government received over £66,000 in Jewish taxation (nearly £4,000 a year); between 1273 and 1278 the annual average was just under £900.[22] No tallages were imposed at all between 1278 and 1287, and the final tallage before the Expulsion, which was assessed at £13,333 in 1287, brought in just under £4,000, a fairly healthy amount. Even taking this into account, however, and assuming that at least some more payments were received for which the records have been lost, Edward I received little more than £10,000 in Jewish taxation between 1272 and 1290. Of course, as a result of the violence of the 1260s and the restrictions imposed on Jewish lenders in 1269 and 1271, there were fewer Jews in England for Edward to tax than there had been for his father. Nevertheless, during the last two decades of its time in England, the evidence is strongly suggestive of a Jewish community in steep financial decline.

And to financial decline was added more vicious persecution in 1278–9. At this time a royal campaign against coin-clipping was launched, and it was the Jews who bore the brunt of the government's actions. Traditionally, indeed since Anglo-Saxon times, the English coinage had been regarded as one of the best in Europe. However, by the late 1270s, many of the current coins had been in circulation for over forty years (the last full recoinage had been in 1247). They had deteriorated to such an extent, one chronicler claimed, that they weighed only half of what they should, with the result that foreign merchants saw little point in coming to England to trade.[23] The poor quality and light weight of the coinage in the 1270s was not just attributable to ordinary wear and tear, however. Many of the coins had been clipped; in other words, small pieces of the coins had been cut off, probably with the aim of accumulating enough clippings to turn into ingots or sheet silver. Another illegal practice was to coat sheets of base metal in the silver which came from the coins and pass them off as solid silver. Clearly there was a strong possibility that trade would be damaged by the poor state of the coinage; but more importantly, the image of kingship was at stake. A strong, stable currency was a mark of a strong, stable government. If the king failed to control his coinage properly, it would reflect badly on his authority. Something would have to be done.

Coin-clipping was a time-honoured practice by the 1270s, then, and there is every reason to believe that both Jews and Christians were involved in the practice.[24] In December 1276, judges were appointed to hear and determine allegations of coin-clipping against Jews and Christians in London and Nottingham.[25] And it is clear that at least some such investigations were carried out. By January 1278, for example, a London Jew, Manser son of Aaron, had been cleared of coin-clipping. Clipped coin had been planted in his house, it seems; or, more specifically, 'a portion of clipped coin, with the forceps employed in clipping it, tied up in a cloth, was maliciously thrown on the top of his house in the City of London and found there, by reason of which he was imprisoned'. On Manser's request, the king appointed a two-man commission to investigate this set-up.[26] A more thoroughgoing effort to deal with debasers of the coinage began later in 1278, however. In November of that year, Jews from across England suspected of coin-clipping were arrested and imprisoned. At least two chroniclers claimed that all of the Jews were seized in this way; another claimed that all of the Jews in England, regardless of their age or sex, were suddenly seized and imprisoned in castles across England before their houses were thoroughly searched.[27] It is certainly hard to believe that every English

Jew was arrested and imprisoned in November 1278, but the number of those detained was almost certainly large. Indeed there is evidence which shows that no less than 600 Jews were imprisoned in the Tower of London for 140 days in 1278–9, and it has been suggested that these may have been the heads of English Jewish households.[28] After the arrests, in January 1279, three groups of judges were commissioned by the government to deal with Jewish and Christian coin-clippers and their accomplices throughout England.[29] The justice meted out to those found guilty, particularly if they were Jewish, was harsh and swift. Brutal punishment for offences against the coinage was not new. As far back as 1124, King Henry I had ordered that all the moneyers in England should have their right hands cut off after he had received complaints from his mercenaries about the quality of the coin with which he was paying them.[30] However, the number of those punished in 1278–9 was very large. One chronicler claimed that 280 Jewish men and women were executed in London alone, and a great many more in other cities. A London chronicler claimed that 293 Jews were hanged, whilst the chronicler at the abbey of Bury St Edmunds claimed that 267 Jews suffered this fate in the capital. Other writers are less specific, but they agree that a large number of Jews were executed for offences against the coinage at this time.[31] Historians have found it difficult to accept these figures, despite their exactness. According to one, 'the estimates of the chroniclers… are not to be taken seriously'.[32] However, recent research by Zefirah Rokeah has shown that they are almost certainly credible: shortly after the arrests, for example, the sheriffs of London and Middlesex received payment for 'doing justice on' (in other words, executing) 269 Jews.[33]

There can be little doubt either that, by early 1279, the campaign against coin-clipping had been transformed into a campaign against the Jews. The relatively small number of Christians who, according to the chroniclers, were hanged

is striking. The same London chronicler who recorded the
deaths of nearly 300 Jews says that only three Christians
were executed. And those officials who were paid for having
executed 269 Jews in 1278–9 also received an allowance for
hanging twenty-nine Christians.[34] There is no reason to think
that Jews were so much more heavily involved in debasing the
coinage than Christians. Indeed, the bulk of the evidence so
far uncovered which deals with offences against the coinage
at this time concerns Christians. But many of them were able
to pay fines to escape more serious punishment, whilst the
proportion of accused Jews who were also able to do this was
much smaller. It is clear that 'religious prejudice was the crucial
factor involved in the degree of punishment'.[35]

The early months of 1279 must therefore have been a time
of great fear and anxiety for the Jews in England, and it is
likely that the government's punitive attitude towards them
encouraged others to further the persecution in less official
ways. By the late spring of 1279, indeed, the government may
have become aware that their anti-Jewish policy was getting
out of hand. On 7 May 1279, an order was issued bringing
the campaign to an end.[36] All those Jews recently convicted
of clipping coin had been executed, the order stated, whilst
others, whose lands and goods had been confiscated, were still
in prison. However, the king had become aware, it went on, of
how 'many Christians, through hatred of the Jews' were con-
cocting accusations against innocent members of the Jewish
community in order to terrify or blackmail them. Therefore,
it had been decided that no Jew would be charged with a
new offence against the coinage unless he had already been
accused before 1 May, and if he made a payment to the king.
Those Jews currently in prison and waiting to be dealt with
could also pay to be released. This act of apparent royal mercy
might suggest that Edward I and his ministers had become
genuinely concerned for the welfare of the Jews by the middle

of 1279. Alternatively, they may have thought that the sums to be collected in fines to secure release or recovery of lands were worth having more than the sums which would be gained from continuing to prosecute alleged coin-clippers. It has been calculated that the government received more than £11,000 between 1278 and 1279 from the sale of the goods and property of condemned Jews.[37] It is likely that by May 1279 there was little more to be squeezed out, and an act of royal clemency would not involve any significant financial loss. However, there may have been other reasons for the issue of the order of 7 May, and an even more sinister background to the events of 1278–9.[38] The available evidence, which has been analysed by Paul Brand, suggests that before the start of the inquiry, in order to ensure convictions against coin-clippers and other abusers of the coinage, the government sent agents around the country buying up silver which had been made from melted-down clippings. One of these undercover operatives was a converted Jew, Henry of Winchester. Henry had been a particular favourite of Henry III; his closeness to Edward's father, indeed, is strongly suggested by the Christian name he took on converting. He was regularly and profitably employed in royal service from at least the early 1250s.[39] In 1278–9, he probably would have been able to collect evidence in both Jewish and Christian communities without arousing too much suspicion. So successful was Henry, indeed, that at one point during his mission he was arrested and imprisoned in Bristol Castle on suspicion of dealing illegally in the plate which he was in fact collecting on royal authority. Those Jews arrested and imprisoned in 1278–9, therefore, 'may well have been the victims of a well-organised "sting" operation'.[40] In other words, the government knew before January 1279 (when the inquiry into coin-clipping was formally begun) the identities of those whom it wanted to arrest because Henry of Winchester had already gathered together the evidence against them. Perhaps this is why there were already 600 Jews in prison by the end of 1278, and also why the coin-clipping campaign was halted in May 1279: 'if the original trials were indeed conducted on the basis of information whose collection the government itself had sponsored they might indeed have had good reason to suppose that any further accusation now made were indeed groundless'.[41]

It would be naïve to think that all of those Jews found guilty and punished during these two years were in fact innocent of the charges brought against them. Members of the community had long been heavily involved in coin-clipping and the activities associated with it.[42] Nevertheless, it is likely that many innocent Jews did suffer unjustly as a result of the activities of men like Henry of Winchester. Edward I must also take his fair share of the blame for the events of 1278–9. As has been seen, it was by his order that they were brought to an end in May 1279; but the king's charitable motivation here is certainly questionable. He also had much to gain financially from the confiscations and fines imposed on the convicted Jews, and it seems that he was personally involved in appointing at least some of those who inquired into the coin-clipping allegations and in giving oral instructions to others who were involved in Jewish affairs at this time. And Henry of Winchester's activities 'must have received approval at the very highest levels of royal government, since it was paid for by the King's wardrobe and the expenses... were specifically approved by the king in person'.[43] Whilst the king's personal involvement in these events is clear, though, the reasons for it are not. He may simply have decided to take a harder line against the Jews. It is just as likely, however, that the need to issue a new coinage motivated him even more. Edward had decided on a recoinage by January 1279. This was a costly business involving the recruitment of moneyers, the manufacture of new dies, the purchase of equipment and the refurbishment of old buildings. New silver also had to be found to begin the recoinage itself.[44] The £11,000 or so which Edward recovered from those Jews found guilty of coinage offences in 1278–9 would have proved very useful. But of course, the anti-Jewish dimension to the events of these years cannot be ignored. Perhaps Edward and his advisers had already begun to realise that their plans to convert the Jews into respectable traders were failing. Thus any suggestion of a more sympathetic or nuanced approach to the Jewish problem was temporarily abandoned in favour of more direct action, and the events of 1278–9 may represent the first signs of a loss of patience with his Jewish subjects on the king's part. It is arguable that the need to reform the coinage provided an excuse to act against the Jews more decisively than before and on the basis that they were simply common criminals who deserved to be punished. Such an argument would have allowed the persecutors to circumvent the Church's ban on forcibly converting the Jews to Christianity; and this, as the terms of the 1275 statute made clear, was a ban which Edward I was not prepared to ignore. Thus, the experience of 1278–9 was a traumatic one for England's Jews: 'it decimated families, dislocated businesses and shattered financial relationships'. Perhaps even more than the Statute of the Jewry of 1275, the coin-clipping trials and their consequences dealt a decisive blow to the wealth, integrity and self-confidence of England's Jewish community.[45]

And it was not just major events such as these which increased the pressure on the English Jews during this period. Attitudes towards them were hardening more generally. Accusations of ritual murder were being made once more, for example. The travelling royal justices assigned to preside over the London eyre of 1276 were ordered to inquire into 'Jews who perpetrated cruelty on Christian boys' (it would be interesting to know whose idea it was to include this instruction), and as a result, early in that year, issues concerning the crucifixion and drowning of a

Christian boy in London during the reign of Henry III surfaced
again. Certain Jews had originally been cleared of involvement
in the affair, but the eyre justices reopened the case and the king
wanted to know why. Within two weeks, the justices had replied
to the king and had clearly convinced him that there was still a
case to answer. Overall in 1276, the justices of the London eyre
found evidence that two boys had been killed by Jews. Then,
two years later, in 1279, at the time of the coin-clipping trials,
Jews in Northampton were hanged after being found guilty of
taking part in the ritual crucifixion of another Christian boy.[46]
There can be no reasonable doubt that these allegations were
fantastic. Of course something awful may really have happened
to the boys in question, but, as in 1144 with William of Norwich,
or the Norwich *cause célèbre* of 1234, or as in 1255 with Little St
Hugh, they may simply have been the victims of tragic accidents
or, perhaps, of abuse perpetrated by Christians. Either way, blam-
ing the Jews was easy and would help to rationalise or cover
up what had actually occurred. And there were incidents in
other parts of the country, too, which indicate that anti-Jewish
feeling was increasing towards the end of the 1270s. In May
1278, for example, a commission was appointed to deal with the
case of Henna, a Nottingham Jewess, 'who lately in the public
market there assaulted Agatha wife of Robert son of Nemek
and assailed her with abusive words, scandalising her and the
Christian people standing round and spitting in her face'. The
evidence suggests that this may have been just the latest chapter
in a long-standing feud between these two women; nevertheless, it is not surprising that festering grievances were erupting
into violence at this time of strain in the relationship between
English Christians and their Jewish neighbours.[47]

The king's involvement in the London case of 1276, and
in the scandal concerning the conversion to Judaism of the
Dominican Robert of Reading in the previous year, showed
once again how prepared he was to take a personal interest

in Jewish affairs.[48] Further examples of this are plentiful. In May 1277, the king appointed a commission 'to enquire of the names of all Jews', to establish where they lived and to see that they were wearing the tabula, which were described as 'a badge in the form of two tablets of yellow felt, six inches long by three wide'. In other words, Edward was ordering a census of England's Jewish population in order to judge whether or not the 1275 statute was being adhered to. This was no small undertaking.[49] Then, about a year later, the king issued orders which were designed to punish Jews who blasphemed against Christianity. Edward wished, 'as befits a catholic prince, to repress such blasphemies'. He was particularly concerned about those Jews who blasphemed 'by saying or doing any detestable or abominable error in blasphemy of the crucifix of the catholic faith or of St. Mary the Virgin or of the church sacraments'. The outrage in Oxford in 1268 may still have been fresh in his memory. Edward also took this opportunity to state once more that Jewish women as well as men should be obliged to wear the tabula (an order which was repeated by him again in December 1281), and he also reiterated many of the conventional strictures against Jews and Christians living together or serving each other. Procedures were also laid down for Christians who wished to recover their pledged belongings from condemned Jews. It may have been as a result of these investigations that the financier Abraham son of Deulecresse was drawn and burned for 'blasphemy and other trespasses' at Norwich in 1279.[50]

At the same time, that Edward was still keen to see the Jews convert even after the events of 1278–9 is suggested by evidence from 1280. On 2 January of that year the king ordered all his local officers to compel the Jews within their jurisdictions to attend sermons preached by Dominicans. There was nothing novel about such an order; they had been issued in other parts of Europe at various points during the thirteenth century, in Aragon by James I in 1242 and by Louis IX in France in 1263, for example.[51] But in the sinister words of the English order of 1280, the royal officers were 'to induce the Jews, by such means as they under the inspiration of the spirit of truth may think most efficient, to assemble and hear without tumult, contention or blasphemy, the word of God preached by the friars, and to see that the rest do not interfere with those who become converted'.[52] And in a similar vein just four months later, with the prospect of conversion very much in his mind, Edward issued new regulations for the administration of the *Domus Conversorum* in London. The principle that all of the goods of a converted Jew were seized by the crown was relaxed. Henceforward, converts would be permitted to keep half of the value of their goods 'in order that those who have already turned from their blindness to the light of the Church may be strengthened in the firmness of their faith, and those who still persist in their error may more willingly and readily turn to the grace of the faith'. These new regulations were issued, the king asserted, because he believed 'that the conversion of Jewish depravity to the Catholic faith would specially be to the increase of faith and worship of the name of Christ'. At the same time, the king also ordered that a priest should be appointed to oversee and manage the *Domus*. He should be assisted by a chaplain, preferably himself a convert.[53]

Taken together, the events of the 1270s display the ambivalent nature of the Edwardian approach to the Jews. On the one hand, the king was prepared to countenance or turn a blind eye to the brutality and violence of 1278–9; yet on the other his desire peacefully to convert the Jews to Christianity and to turn them away from usury towards less sinful trading activities seems to have been quite genuine and heartfelt. What should be done with the Jews was clearly an issue which concerned the king, and, as has been seen, it was one to which he regularly returned. But whilst his own feelings about the

Jews must have dictated the course of government policy, he did not act in a vacuum; and it is worth thinking about the influences on Edward which led him to act as he did. Of course, his family was important in shaping his outlook, and the dealings of Edward's close relatives with the Jews must have made him aware of both the benefits and the perils of such involvement. Edward cannot have failed to take account of his father's increasingly aggressive attitude towards the Jews. By contrast, however, his uncle, Richard of Cornwall, had a long history of dealings with the Jews, much of which was sensitive and relatively enlightened.[54] The king's brother, Edmund, Earl of Lancaster, was also deeply involved in Jewish affairs. By 1269 he had been 'given' his own Jew, Aaron son of Vives, by Henry III. Thereafter, Aaron performed the role of 'bond-broker to the prince' and the rolls of the Chancery and the Exchequer are full of grants and concessions to him, most of which were designed to allow him to transact business freely and most of which were secured by his royal patron. The cloak of protection draped around Aaron's shoulders by Edmund allowed the former to become one of the richest and most influential Jews in London by the time of the Expulsion.[55]

The women in Edward's life cannot have failed to influence him either. The anti-Jewish views of the king's mother, Eleanor of Provence, have long been thought to have had a decisive impact on her son's policies. One chronicler even went so far as to claim that the Expulsion of 1290 was Eleanor's idea. However, there is no other evidence to support this charge, or the view that Queen Eleanor was unusually hostile to the Jews.[56] To be sure, Eleanor had the Jews on her dower lands expelled in 1275, and there is no reason to think that she liked Jews, associated with them more than she had to or had any sympathy for their beliefs or their predicament. In these respects, however, Eleanor was hardly extreme by the standards of her own time. She was involved in the trafficking of Jewish debts like many of her contemporaries, and she was even prepared to secure grants and privileges for certain Jews when it suited her to do so.[57] Edward's first wife, Eleanor of Castile, was even more heavily involved with Jewish finance than his mother. Like her brother-in-law Edmund of Lancaster, Eleanor held certain Jews in special favour, none more so than the London Jew Cok Hagin, or Hagin son of Cresse, who, 'at the instance of Eleanor, the king's consort, and with the assent of the commonalty of the Jews of England', was appointed archpresbyter in May 1281.[58] He was the nephew of the previous archpresbyter, Hagin, whose time in office had been dogged by accusations that, after the London massacre of 1264, he had concealed the death of an infant child of one of the victims, Cok son of Aaron. Hagin was imprisoned several times before his death in 1280. Meanwhile, in 1275, Cok Hagin was excommunicated by another of his uncles and Hagin's brother, the great Jewish scholar Master Elias, after which Eleanor was granted all his debts and chattels. In the 1280s, Cok was little more than Eleanor's financial agent, and he was instrumental in furthering many of the queen's land acquisitions.[59] And indeed, her appetite for land was notorious even amongst contemporaries: 'the king covets our money/and the queen our lovely manors', as one piece of thirteenth-century doggerel had it.[60] And much of this land came from grants to her of Jewish debts by her husband. Often she would seek repayment of the loans she acquired in this way, but Eleanor was just as happy taking possession of the lands pledged as security for the loans.[61] She 'had emerged by 1281 as one of the most active acquisitors of encumbered estates in the kingdom'.[62] Edward had found a relatively cheap way of providing for his wife, and Eleanor was happy to go along with it. Perhaps her own attitude towards the Jews was more relaxed than that of her English relatives. Having been brought up in Castile, where Jews were more numerous and more integrated into Christian society than in England, the anti-Jewish sentiment she encountered there after her arrival in the 1250s may have startled her. This is not to suggest that Eleanor of Castile liked Jews any more than Eleanor of Provence did, however: 'the sole reason for her relations with them was that they offered a convenient means to secure land or cash'.[63]

Eleanor of Castile's involvement with Jewish finance was controversial because she was, in effect, profiting from usury on an extensive scale. In about 1283 the archbishop of Canterbury, John Pecham, wrote to her in strident terms, reminding her that usury was 'a mortal sin to those who take the usury and those who support it, and those who have a share in it'. It seems that the queen took little notice, however, because at the end of 1286 Pecham wrote another letter, this time to the keeper of Eleanor's wardrobe. Scandalous rumours were circulating, he said, that the queen was still acquiring estates which had been pledged as security for usurious transactions. 'There is public outcry and gossip about this in every part of England', the archbishop complained, and it was time for the queen to end her involvement in such detestable practices.[64] It was Pecham indeed 'who spearheaded the religious campaign against both usury and the Jews' in England; and certainly a freshly intolerant tone was introduced into the official views of the English Church on the Jews after he became archbishop of Canterbury in 1279.[65] Edward I cannot have failed to notice this or the attitude of others amongst his bishops. During the Easter parliament of 1285, the bishops of the Canterbury province presented several sets of grievances to the king, included amongst which was a plea for the enforcement of the prohibition of usury (an interesting comment on the effectiveness of the legislation of 1275), and another urging the Jews to be made to take part in manual labour or lawful trade.[66] It is not surprising, therefore, that when, in 1286, Richard Swinfield, Bishop of Hereford discovered that Christians had attended a

Jewish wedding in his diocese, he warned that they would be excommunicated unless they secured absolution immediately. Such outrage was representative of the hardening views of the English ecclesiastical hierarchy towards the Jews, although it is also strongly suggestive of the view that, left to themselves, Jews and Christians were more than capable of interacting and coexisting quite peacefully.[67]

As for Pecham, it should come as no surprise that his views on the Jews were so aggressively hostile. As head of the English Church, he must have thought that it was his responsibility to set an example. But just as much as he was an archbishop, Pecham was also a Franciscan, and the members of this order as well as their fellow mendicants the Dominicans, with their emphasis on preaching, conversion and poverty, had always taken a particular interest in the Jews, their beliefs and their practices. It has been seen already that it was Dominican preachers whom the Jews were compelled by royal order to go and hear in 1280. And prior to this, in September 1272, only a month after Edward had returned to England after his crusade, an order was issued for the closure of the Jews' principal London synagogue, on the east side of Colechurch Lane, following a request from a neighbouring community of friars. The Jews, it seems, were making such a noise during their worship that the friars could not carry out their own services properly. Having been given royal consent to build a new synagogue (special permission was required because the construction of new synagogues had been prohibited by Henry III in 1253), the Jews were forced to abandon their Colechurch Lane site. By the early 1280s, a new location on the south side of Catte Street had been found; but Archbishop Pecham was unhappy with what he had heard about the Jews' building plans. His initial impulse was to try and stop the construction of the new synagogue completely, and he wrote to the bishop of London, Richard Gravesend, in July 1281 ordering him to intervene. Given what had been agreed in 1272, however, Pecham's efforts were unsuccessful. Nevertheless, this did not prevent him writing to Gravesend again in August of the following year, this time ordering him to shut down all the private synagogues he had heard were being used in London. He eventually conceded, however, in a third letter, that the Jews could have a new communal synagogue, as long as it was small.[68] Now there is little direct evidence to suggest that Edward I was a particularly enthusiastic supporter either of Pecham personally (the two were frequently at odds over the relationship between the lay and ecclesiastical powers) or of the friars more generally. He regularly gave the latter alms, but they were by no means the only recipients of his charity.[69] However, the king cannot have been immune to their obvious spirituality. For one thing, he would have heard about them from his relatives. Henry III's confessor during the 1250s and 1260s, John of Darlington, was a Dominican 'with a personal mission to the Jews'; and both Eleanor of Provence and Eleanor of Castile were keen and active supporters of the mendicant orders.[70] And Edward's esteem for them is brought into focus for a moment by an incident which took place in 1277. In that year, a Jew named Sampson was accused of having dressed himself up as a Franciscan and preached against the order and the Christian faith. The archbishop of Canterbury, Robert Kilwardby (himself a Dominican; he was succeeded by Pecham in 1279), heard about the case and ordered that Sampson should be driven naked for three days in succession through Oxford, London, Northampton, Lincoln and Canterbury, with the entrails of a calf in his hands and its flayed body around his neck. Initially the sheriff of Northamptonshire refused to carry out these grotesque orders without royal instructions, only to be told that the king himself supported them. In doing so, Edward was attempting to preserve the dignity of the mendicant orders whilst at the same time safeguarding Christian orthodoxy through an expression of his distaste for the Jews.[71]

Of course, the friars were not influential just in England, and across Europe at this time they were known to act as the mouthpieces of official Church policy on the Jews.[72] This policy certainly showed signs of becoming more belligerent in the 1270s and 1280s. In the early 1270s, Pope Gregory X (1271–6) restated the long-standing view that the Jews should not be forcibly converted; but during his pontificate, too, in 1274, the Council of Lyons's strictures against usury can only have served to toughen the orthodox line. And it was in response to the papal bull *Vineam Sorec* of 1278 that Edward I announced in 1280 that all Jews were to hear Dominican sermons. And in 1286, in spite of their efforts to address Jewish issues in parliament in the previous year, the archbishops of Canterbury and York were reprimanded by Pope Honorius IV for what he saw as the laxity of their approach. He condemned the amount of contact that he understood took place between Christians and Jews, and he denounced the continuing study of the Talmud as a threat to Christian beliefs.[73] The papal criticism of the English bishops was unfair, however; there was little they could do in the absence of a consistent royal policy.

With such opinions and beliefs in the air during the 1270s and 1280s, it is impossible to believe that Edward I was not influenced by them. His own policies towards the Jews, inconsistent as they were, were based on the fundamental hostility he felt towards them and their religion. However, even though it has been suggested that, 'under Edward I, the impression of a deliberate and calculated embrace of anti-Semitism is hard to avoid', there is nothing to suggest that the fate of England's Jews had already been decided upon by the middle of the 1280s.[74] Indeed, what evidence there is suggests that Edward and his advisers were still striving to find a balanced solution to the Jewish problem at that time. A draft statute, which probably dates from the period 1284–6, seems to acknowledge that the Statute of Jewry's attempt to turn the Jews into legitimate traders had failed.[75] Remarkably, however, the draft also envisaged allowing the Jews to return to lending money at interest, albeit subject to strict controls on the rates of interest charged and on the way the loans were contracted. There is nothing to indicate that this statute ever came into force; but that it was drafted at all shows how flexible, or perhaps contradictory, the approach of the Edwardian government towards the Jews could be. Nobody, it seems, really knew what the best line of attack was, whether it should be tough or tender, violent or coaxing. Usury was continuing, however, and if the demand for it meant that it was bound to do so even in the face of the government's attempts to prevent it, perhaps there were those within the royal administration who thought it would be better to regulate the practice than see it go further underground. Whatever the reality, however, it is clear that, when Edward I left England in 1286 for a three-year stay on the continent, there were still alternatives to expulsion. Indeed, it is not at all clear whether the option of expulsion had even been considered by Edward when he set sail from Dover on 13 May 1286.

6

Expulsion

B y the time Edward I left England for France in May 1286, the number of Jews in England had dwindled. Estimates vary, but there were almost certainly no more than 4,000 Jews in the kingdom by the 1280s, and it is much more likely that there were as few as 2,000.[1] These Jews have traditionally been seen as the sad rump of a once thriving community; in the words of Cecil Roth, for example, by 1290 England's remaining Jews had been 'reduced to the lowest depth of misery and degradation'.[2] The evidence for this is compelling. As has been seen, during the middle third of the thirteenth century, the royal government had systematically milked the English Jewish community of the bulk of its wealth. During the civil war of the 1260s, English Jews had suffered persecution at the hands of partisans, bigots and opportunists. Then, in the late 1260s and 1270s, a series of ordinances culminating in the Statute of Jewry of 1275, followed by the coin-clipping trials and subsequent executions and confiscations, had only served to kick the Jewish community hardest when it was already down.

Many Jews who had seen their friends and relatives ruined, murdered or executed during this period would surely have seen little point remaining in England, and they may have left the kingdom of their own accord. And so, superficially at least, there is every reason to think that, in the second half of the 1280s, England's Jewish community was a sorry shadow of its former self. Indeed, such views have been at the centre of most interpretations of the Expulsion of 1290. Financially exhausted and numerically insignificant, the Jews of mid-Edwardian England were dispensable. The king had more to gain both politically and financially from expelling them than from continuing to protect them.

The persuasive response to this long-established view provided by the recent work of Robin Mundill has already been mentioned.[3] He has suggested that not all was hopeless for those Jews who had been able to survive the onslaught and adapt to the changes of the 1270s.[4] The picture in the decades prior to the Expulsion, he has argued, was not one of universal decay and financial collapse across the whole of English Jewry. Some Jews appear to have succeeded in becoming legitimate traders by involving themselves in the provision of advance credit on the sale of wool and cereals.[5] Of course there were casualties, and not all Jews profited equally by any means. But at Lincoln, Hereford and Canterbury during Edward I's reign, and in other smaller communities across the kingdom, Jewish business survived until the eve of the Expulsion, and, in the hands of some traders, it thrived. Mundill concludes: 'it is not easy to state firmly that the Edwardian Anglo-Jewry was a business community in decline [and] the traditional explanations of why Edward I decided to banish the Jews in 1290 may have to be re-examined'.[6] There are various problems with the evidence used to reach these conclusions. It is very difficult to interpret convincingly one way or another, and, although Mundill addresses this criticism head-on and with conviction, it is still hard to

ignore the likelihood that many of the agreements which purported to stipulate the repayment of Jewish credit in the form of
wool or corn were in fact fictitious transactions cloaking usury.[7]
This is what the draft statute of *c*.1284–6, which was discussed
at the end of the previous chapter, thought was happening,
and, as will be seen, it was the alleged failure of the Jews to
abandon usury which provided the official basis for expulsion in
1290. Also, the relative penury of England's Jewish community
during Edward I's reign as demonstrated by the records of its
tallage payments has already been discussed.[8] Between 1272 and
1290, only something in the region of £9,300 was collected by
the royal government, compared with nearly £75,000 between
1241 and 1256. That tallage payments on any significant scale
at all were produced in the 1270s and 1280s shows that there
was still financial life in the English Jewish community. And
there is no reason to doubt either that Jewish trading went on
consistently until 1290 or that individual Jews did not profit
as a result. Nevertheless, evidence from the Jewish community
in York suggests that at least one major provincial Jewry was
in a state of ongoing social and financial collapse during the
1270s and 1280s.[9] And more generally, it remains hard to avoid
the conclusion that, in financial terms, England's Jews were
struggling to cope by 1290. Whenever thoughts of expulsion
first occurred to him, therefore, Edward I 'could afford to be
influenced by "religious" considerations'.[10]

The financial plight of England's Jews may have been brought
home to the royal government with fatal force when an attempt
was made to levy a tallage in 1287. No such tax had been
raised since 1278, and perhaps it was thought that, after having
been given nearly a decade to recover from the last demand,
the Jews would now be in a position to respond productively
to the king's needs. If this was the hope, however, it was soon
disappointed. According to some chronicles, the tallage itself
was assessed at the very large sum of £13,333, the same as in

1241. But where that tallage had brought over £9,000 into the royal coffers, in 1287 it seems that only just less than £4,000 was actually collected. This was by no means an insignificant sum; but it appears to have been extracted only under the most intense pressure. On 2 May 1287, all the leading Jews in England were arrested and imprisoned, and they were released only after having promised to pay the king £12,000.[11] And for Edward's ministers, who were administering the tallage in their master's absence, the ever-diminishing returns from the Jewry must have been striking. The efforts involved in collecting such relatively insignificant sums were coming to outweigh the financial benefits of continuing to do so. It is right to say, therefore, that 'in expelling [the Jews] from the country Edward was hardly depriving himself of a substantial source of future revenue'.[12]

Indeed, by 1290, the Jews had long since lost their place as the first financiers of the kingdom. Henry III had borrowed money from Italian merchants to fund his foreign adventures, but Edward I used their resources much more systematically than his father had done. Until 1294 it was the firm of the Riccardi of Lucca which advanced most money to the crown, over £200,000 in the first seven years of the reign alone. All but £23,000 of this was repaid, in part with the customs revenues Edward I was granted in 1275.[13] This was a much more regular and reliable system of financial supply than the Jews had ever been able to provide. And it was not just the king who used Italian financiers either. They lent money to individuals and institutions, lay and ecclesiastical, from different levels of English society, as, by the end of the thirteenth century, did other Christian English lenders. Many of these men were high-ranking royal servants who were able to use their influence and the administrative mechanisms at their disposal to have their debts enrolled on official government records and their payment enforced.[14] There had always been Christian money-lenders in England operating alongside Jewish ones, and there is still strength in the view that 'to suggest that in England the Jews were replaced by Italians is to misconceive the course of history'.[15] After all, the Italians, whose loans were in large measure repaid, had a very different relationship with their royal patron than did the Jews, who could be taxed at will by the king. Nevertheless, it is only reasonable to think that people would have sought out alternative sources of credit as the worsening financial condition of the English Jews became more apparent. This in turn would only have made that condition worse still. By 1290 Jewish financial services, even had they been available on a significant scale, were no longer required as they once had been either by the king, the Church, the magnates or the gentry. They all had other options, whilst those still in debt to Jewish creditors would have been happy to see them go. On the eve of the Expulsion, therefore, there was simply no influential constituency with a vested interest in the maintenance of a Jewish presence in England.

Even this, however, did not make expulsion inevitable. In 1286, the Jewish community in England was just as likely to wither away as be exterminated. However, a hardening of Edward I's own religious views late in that year or early in the next appears to have begun the final phase of existence for England's medieval Jewry. Whilst travelling south from Paris, where he had performed homage to the new French king, Philip IV, for his duchy of Gascony in June 1286, Edward fell ill. Precisely what the nature of this illness was is unclear, but it appears to have been serious. And it may have been during this illness that the king vowed to go on crusade again (a promise he never fulfilled), probably in the late spring of 1287.[16] It may also have been because of a heightened religious sensibility that Edward ordered the expulsion of the Jews from Gascony at the end of that year.[17] Jews there were speedily arrested and their property was confiscated before they were actually expelled. The king and his collectors were then quick to try and enforce payment of the debts which had come into their hands. It is this haste to collect the cash which has persuaded some historians to see Edward's motives in expelling the Gascon Jews as purely financial. 'No special pleading can cloak Edward's action in Gascony with the garb of piety or justice', Richardson said.[18]

And to be sure, Edward was in particular need of funds in 1287, as the extremity of the methods used by his agents in England to collect the Jewish tallage assessed in that year suggests. Edward was desperate to secure the release from captivity in Aragon of his cousin (their mothers were sisters), Charles of Salerno.[19] Charles was the son of Charles I of Anjou, the ruler of the kingdom of Sicily until he was ousted in 1282 as a result of the War of the Sicilian Vespers. It was in the aftermath of this conflict that Charles of Salerno had been captured and confined by the Aragonese, whose kings, first Peter III (d.1285) and then Alphonso III (d.1291), claimed the Sicilian throne through marriage. Edward I found himself caught between the warring crowns of France and Aragon, as vassal of the former on the one hand, and as the father of Eleanor, the intended bride of Peter, the heir to the Aragonese throne, on the other. In July 1287, therefore, the English king met his Aragonese counterpart and they agreed that Charles would be released on the payment of 50,000 marks which, in 1288, Edward agreed to pay himself. Historians have tended to be surprised by Edward's readiness to enter into such a one-sided bargain. It was certainly an extraordinary decision, an act of folly more characteristic of Henry III than Edward I. Perhaps Edward was genuinely concerned for Charles. This is certainly what Powicke thought: 'there must be few parallels in history to this comprehensive gesture by a great king on behalf of a friend', he said.[20] More pragmatic, perhaps, was Edward's urgent desire to see his daughter's marriage, and his even more pressing wish to go on crusade, a plan for which peace in Europe was an essential prerequisite. Certainly, the deal Edward struck with Alphonso smacks of desperation and a certain naivety about how difficult it would be to raise the funds involved. For one historian, therefore, the link between the Gascon expulsion and the ransom agreement was clear: Edward I's motive for expelling the Gascon Jews was 'quite blatantly the acquisition of their assets by a king hard pressed to raise the funds needed to obtain the release of his cousin, Charles of Salerno, from captivity'.[21] However, the connection between the Expulsion and the ransom is not so clear-cut. For one thing, Edward did not agree to pay the ransom himself until nearly a year after the Gascon Jews had been expelled. What is more, Edward does not appear to have profited significantly from the Gascon expulsion in any event. Most of the sums recovered from the liquidation of the Jews' assets were distributed as alms to the mendicant orders in Aquitaine. And many of the debts which did come into the king's hands were recovered only in part, a deliberate act of royal policy.[22] The idea that the Gascon expulsion was intended as a money-raising exercise, therefore, is clearly wrong. Much more convincing is the idea that the Expulsion was intended as a genuine thank-offering for Edward's recovery from illness. Whatever the king's motives, however, the Gascon episode gave Edward his first experience of expulsion on a significant scale. It had demonstrated what could be done.

Of course the idea of expulsion was not new to England in the late 1280s. As far back as the 1180s, Roger of Asterby, a Lincolnshire knight indebted to Aaron of Lincoln, after having received his instructions to try and persuade the king to do this directly from St Peter and the archangel Gabriel, had told Henry II to expel the Jews from his lands.[23] King Henry took no notice, but soon after, in 1190, the abbot of Bury St Edmunds did expel the Jews from his lands with royal permission.[24] A century later, Edward I may not have known of these events, but he is more likely to have been familiar with many of the local expulsions which had taken place in England during the thirteenth century. His own uncle, Simon de Montfort, had expelled the Jews from Leicester in 1231, and other expulsions had taken place subsequently at Warwick and Newcastle in 1234, High Wycombe in 1235, and Southampton in 1236. And within Edward's lifetime, expulsions had continued regularly to take place, at Berkhampstead in 1242 and at Newbury in 1244.[25] Then, in 1261, the burgesses of Derby were granted permission by Henry III to exclude Jews from their town, and in 1266 the abbess of Romsey secured a royal grant to the effect that no Jews should dwell in that town either. In a similar vein, Jews were ordered out of Winchelsea and Bridgnorth in June 1273 and October 1274 respectively, because these were not authorised places of Jewish settlement; and in 1275, of course, Edward had granted his own mother permission to exclude Jews from her dower lands.[26] Nor can Edward have been unaware of larger-scale continental examples of expulsion. In 1182, King Philip II of France had expelled all Jews from his demesne lands, and Louis IX had attempted something similar in 1248 or 1249. Meanwhile, Duke John of Brittany had ordered all Jews to leave his duchy in 1239.[27] Such events would have meant that the possibility of expulsion always remained apparent to Edward I. But one example of expulsion may have influenced him above all others.

Having finally been freed from captivity in October 1288, Charles of Salerno expelled the Jews from his counties of Maine and Anjou. And in a document dated 8 December 1289, he explained why.[28] He had found 'numerous Jews... dwelling randomly and publicly among Christians', and, to make matters worse, 'they evilly cohabit with many Christian maidens'. In expelling them, Charles admitted, he would suffer a loss of 'temporal profit'; but he preferred 'to provide for the peace of our subjects than to fill our coffers with the mammon of iniquity'. Charles tried to be fair, too: as well as expelling the Jews, he expelled from Maine and Anjou 'all Lombards, Cahorsins and other foreigners who engage in public usury'. However, the edict of expulsion also made it quite clear that Charles was to be granted a tax by the grateful people of Maine and Anjou 'as some recompense for the profit which we lose through the aforesaid expulsions'. In this case, therefore, the link between expulsion and the grant of a tax was explicit. Perhaps Charles was building on the precedent set by Edward I in Gascony in 1287. In turn, perhaps Edward I learned something from his cousin's approach. Grants of taxation in England had been linked to the implementation of statutory limitations on Jewish trading activity in 1269 and 1275. In 1289–90, however, it must have become clear to Edward that expulsion itself, the greatest concession of them all, could be profitable as well as popular and pious.

When he returned to England in August 1289, however, expelling the Jews was probably the last thing on Edward's mind. The costs of maintaining an itinerant court abroad for three years had been high, and the revenues from Gascony had never been sufficient to meet the king's expenses whilst he had been on the continent. As a result, Edward was heavily in debt to his Italian financiers.[29] And by 1289, of course, he had also undertaken to contribute the major part of Charles of Salerno's ransom. Whilst still in France, in February 1288, the king's request for a tax had been turned down by his magnates, who were not prepared to grant a subsidy unless the king asked for it in person.[30] In 1289, therefore, Edward's financial situation was worrying. But so was the state of the kingdom; and just as he had been as the returning crusader in 1274, so the king was bent on reforming and reinvigorating it. In October 1289 at London an assembly of magnates was summoned to meet early in 1290, and a proclamation was issued inviting those with grievances against royal officials to appear at Westminster in November. The inquiries and hearings which eventually resulted from this proclamation were to last until 1293, and some great men, judges and royal officials, fell from grace as a result. However, Edward's aim in launching this inquisition was not to attack them so much as his lesser officials in the localities: his intention was 'to improve the king's image in the countryside, an important step in preparing for the upcoming parliamentary negotiations over taxation'.[31]

Edward also managed to make some money, perhaps as much as £30,000, from the confiscations and penalties imposed on those found guilty of wrongdoing during the trials.[32] However, such a windfall did not provide enough to solve the king's more deep-seated financial problems. Only a tax granted by parliament could do this. However, the assembly which gathered at Westminster in January and February 1290 never discussed the question of taxation; other business dominated. Another summons was issued, therefore, for a parliament to meet at Easter.[33] The king spent the first weeks of this parliament getting the magnates on his side, and he began to do this by bringing an end to the so-called *quo warranto* ('by what authority') inquiries which had been underway since 1278. The hundred roll investigations in 1274 had shown that there were serious doubts over many of the claims made by magnates that they were entitled to exercise certain types of jurisdiction over their lands – the right to prevent certain people hunting on those lands, for example, or the right to hear certain types of case in a court of their own. Everyone who claimed rights such as these 'held something which in principle belonged to the king', and so the king's concern was that magnates had simply taken over the exercise of royal rights without royal permission at some undefined point in the past.[34] In 1278, therefore, the king announced that anyone claiming such rights should set out the basis of their claim and prove *quo warranto* they did so. Many magnates simply claimed their rights because nobody could remember a time when they and their predecessors had not exercised them; others had royal charters which purported to prove their entitlement. However, there were long disputes in many cases, and by 1290 there was a serious backlog.[35] Finally, at the Easter parliament of 1290, the king drew some sort of a line under the main issues: in his statute of *quo warranto*, it was announced that anyone who could show that he and his ancestors had exercised the rights they claimed continuously since 1189 could have them confirmed. This dulled the sharpness of magnate grievances and made them more amenable to Edward's request for a tax; and on 29 May Edward received their consent to a 'feudal aid' for the marriage of his eldest daughter, Joan, to the earl of Gloucester. Edward was quite entitled to demand this tax as of right (any feudal lord could do so when his eldest daughter was married), but the fact that he thought it necessary to obtain magnate consent to it shows how reliant he was on their goodwill. He must have been frustrated, too, because it still did not provide enough money to meet his financial needs. He did not even bother to try and collect the aid for over ten years.[36] His concessions of 1290 had got him only so far, and he must have realised that more decisive steps needed to be taken. On 14 June, therefore, the knights of the shire were summoned to attend parliament at Westminster by 15 July.[37]

Four days after the date of this summons, Edward took action against the Jews. On 18 June 1290 he issued secret, unenrolled orders to his sheriffs instructing them to seal the *archae* in their counties on 28 June. There has been much discussion of these orders.[38] For Richardson, they revealed that 'the decision to expel the Jews from England and to confiscate their houses and their bonds must have been taken by the beginning of June 1290'. And most recently, Mundill, whilst not supporting this interpretation completely, has described the issue of the orders of 18 June as 'a necessary prelude to the final official edict of Expulsion'.[39] Stacey and Dobson, by contrast, view the orders very differently. They suggest that, far from showing that Edward I had already decided to expel the Jews by mid-June 1290, they only reveal the king's plan to raise a new Jewish tallage. The sealing of the *archae* was 'standard procedure' at such a time, Stacey argues, and the precise terms of the orders themselves are properly intelligible only if Edward was preparing to collect a new tax. Moreover, royal letters were issued to the Justices of the Jews on 9 July ordering them not to take any action against the chattels of certain Jews 'by reason of any tallage'. This is not conclusive proof that a tallage was planned, but neither do these letters support the idea that expulsion was by then certain.[40]

It is Stacey's firmly-held view, indeed, that expulsion did not become a certainty until after the knights of the shire had begun to arrive at Westminster in the second week of July 1290. After they had gathered, 'what the Commons representatives demanded as the price for their consent to the king's tax was the expulsion of the Jews from England'.[41] Unfortunately, there is no formal record of parliamentary proceedings which confirms this view, and it is just as likely that it was Edward who raised the possibility of expulsion in an effort to tempt the knights into granting a tax. Whoever mentioned it first, however, contemporary chroniclers made either a direct or implied link between the Expulsion and the grant of the tax.[42] And the rapid speed of events after the arrival of the knights gives further support to this interpretation. By 18 July, when orders concerning the Expulsion were issued to the sheriffs, the decision had already been taken: the Jews had been given a certain amount of time to leave the kingdom, the king said (they were all to leave by 1 November 1290, according to one chronicle), and the sheriffs were ordered to make sure that they were not attacked or injured whilst preparing themselves for departure or whilst travelling to the ports.[43]

The final decision to expel the Jews from England, therefore, was taken quickly and without warning. It was taken first and foremost for financial reasons, and Edward I profited significantly as a result. The tax he was granted by parliament in July 1290 was assessed at £116,346, and the amount collected probably fell only a little short of this; it was 'the largest single tax of the Middle Ages'.[44] The English clergy also granted the king a tax of a tenth later in 1290 because the Expulsion of the Jews had pleased them so greatly.[45] The Jewish tallage which Edward had been planning to levy in June 1290 would have been insignificant by comparison, and the future prospect of ever-smaller tallages being levied on an increasingly destitute English Jewry cannot have been enticing. In financial terms Edward had much to gain and little to lose by expelling the Jews.

But there was surely much more to the Expulsion of 1290 than a snap decision made in return for the promise of a single, albeit lucrative, tax. In November 1290, after all of the Jews had left England, Edward set out his reasons for having expelled them. It was their unwillingness to abide by the terms of the Statute of Jewry of 1275 and their persistence in practising usury contrary to the king's commands which had sealed their fate, he said.[46] And indeed, as has been seen, there is every reason to think that Jews had continued to lend money at interest in the fifteen years prior to their banishment. How serious this problem really was, though, is another question. For one thing, as the number of Jews in England had fallen from the mid-thirteenth century, so must the number of Jewish lenders. By 1290, there were probably no more than 2,000 Jews in the kingdom, and it is by no means clear how many of these were involved in the provision of credit. What is more, the changing social background of the Jews' debtors is suggestive of a financial community in decline. At the height of their prosperity, Jewish lenders numbered the great men of Church and state amongst their clients. However, as their wealth had been systematically siphoned away by the government during the mid-thirteenth century, their ability to lend large sums to wealthy men and institutions had been significantly impaired. By the 1270s, Jewish lending was 'overwhelmingly small-scale, rural and short-term'. Small sums were being lent locally to small men; 'short term loans to peasants and craftsmen' were often all that a Jewish lender could manage.[47] This does not mean that there were no Jewish debtors of more exalted social status in 1290; clearly there were in Herefordshire, for example, and in Lincolnshire approximately 17 per cent of the total value of the debts registered in the Lincoln *archa* in 1290 were owed by knights.[48] These men, with their vested interest in the removal of their creditors, were just the sort whose support for taxation Edward I was so keen to secure in July 1290. For them, Jewish lending was still a current and acute problem, and expulsion would have been an attractive solution. However, for Edward I to suggest in November 1290 that usury remained so widespread and serious a threat that it alone justified expulsion was more than a little disingenuous. If Jewish lending had remained such a concern after 1275, then why was no decisive action taken prior to July 1290? Or, indeed, why was the government toying with the idea of allowing Jews to lend at interest again as late as the mid-1280s?

There was more than an element of special pleading to the king's arguments in late 1290, then. But this was not the last time Edward took advantage of popular feelings about the Jews, both to reinforce his own righteous credentials and to score a few political points. Some time in either 1299 or 1300, the king visited the shrine of Little St Hugh at Lincoln Cathedral and made an offering. There was nothing unusual about this in itself, save that this shrine was one for which Edward appears to have had more than conventional enthusiasm. Planned during the first half of the 1290s, although perhaps not completed until after 1303, the shrine's stylistic similarities to the Eleanor Crosses, especially the one at Waltham, have led to suggestions that the same designer, sculptor and master-mason were responsible for both. Moreover, Edward's desire expressly to associate the shrine with the crown, and to identify himself with the cult of Little St Hugh, extended to having his own insignia (shields bearing three leopards), carved and painted on it. In so doing, he was reminding people how the royal stamp of approval had originally been given to the ritual murder myth by Henry III in the aftermath of Hugh's death. He thereby re-emphasised the criminality of the Jews who were believed to have killed him and stressed once more his own role as protector of Christian orthodoxy. Again, there is no reason to think that Edward was dishonest or crudely opportunistic about any of this. Nevertheless, there is little doubt that, as in 1290 albeit on a smaller scale, he wanted to take advantage of popular prejudice against the Jews to further his own political ends and add some virtuous lustre to his image.[49] Once expulsion had taken place, therefore, Edward was quick to try and justify his treatment of the Jews in ways which demonstrated what he wished people to see as the legitimacy and sincerity of his motives. Blinkered, bigoted and unsophisticated as Edward was in this context, the suggestion that he had expelled the Jews for purely financial reasons would probably have offended him.

And to be sure, Edward may have felt genuinely disappointed and frustrated in 1290 by what he perceived as the failure of his Jewish 'experiment'. In his view, in being handed the opportunity to trade legitimately with Christians, the Jews had been given a chance to adapt and survive after 1275; and they had thrown it away by continuing to practise usury. His attempts to encourage conversion to Christianity had also met with little success, it seems. Indeed, the number of Jewish conversions to Christianity in England appears to have declined significantly during Edward's reign. There is no reason to doubt, therefore, that in July 1290 Edward was guided to some extent by 'his sincere religious bigotry'.[50] It has already been seen how he must have been aware of the developing views of the Church towards the Jews. And his prejudice may have been hardened further just prior to his negotiations with parliament. On 28 April 1290 Edward visited his mother at the convent she had settled in at Amesbury in Wiltshire. Eleanor of Provence had taken the veil there in 1286, and she died and was buried at Amesbury in 1291. Famously, of course, one chronicler claimed that expelling the Jews was Eleanor's idea. As has been seen already, this is unlikely. Nevertheless, and given such opinions about the Queen Mother's influence over her son, it is fascinating to speculate on the sort of conversation Edward might have had with his mother less than three months before the Expulsion of the Jews.[51] Whatever they discussed, however, it is quite unrealistic to think that Edward I would have taken such a drastic step unless he thought it was in his own best, most worldly interests. If the Jews had still been a productive and reliable source of regular finance in 1290, then whatever Edward thought about their beliefs, it is not credible to believe that he would have expelled them on exclusively religious grounds. Edward may have been pious, but he was not foolish. And in the end, as Peter Elman has said, 'the Jews were expelled from England because from an economic point of view they were no longer performing that function which was their sole *raison d'être* in the circumstances'.[52] After the event the king claimed to have had religious motives for expelling the Jews, and it would be unfair to suggest that he was not in some way sincere about this.[53] Nevertheless, this cloak of royal piety surely covered a more naked body of pragmatic calculation. The recipe for expulsion contained many more earthly ingredients than spiritual ones; or, as Richardson elegantly put it, in 1290 'Edward's conscience had been stirred by his financial necessities'.[54]

When the Jews were ordered out of England in July 1290, they were given just over three months to leave. All Saints' Day, 1 November, had been fixed as the day by which they had to depart. How this news was communicated to the Jewish communities across England is unclear. The royal commands would probably have been read out in the synagogues and it is likely that word of what had happened spread quickly amongst Jews

and Christians alike. There is no evidence either to show what
the Jews themselves felt about their impending banishment.
Whether they were angry about their treatment or wearily
resigned to it is simply unknown. They were allowed to take
their chattels with them when they left, but had to return to
their debtors any pledges they still retained. Their registered
bonds and landed property would fall to the king, however, who,
for his part, appears to have been keen to enforce the Expulsion
'with superficial fairness, and almost humanity'.[55] On 27 July
1290, safe conducts for the Jews were sent to the authorities
in the Cinque Ports, and in the weeks that followed several of
the better-connected Jews were the subject of royal orders of
their own. Aaron son of Vives, for example, whose relationship
with the king's brother Edmund has been mentioned before,
was given royal permission to sell his houses in London and
elsewhere to any Christian he chose. And on 1 September
Cok Hagin, the archpresbyter and 'Jew of the King's Consort
[Eleanor of Castile]', was also granted permission by the king
and his wife to sell some of his houses in London to Christians.[56]
Meanwhile, the Jews of York who were leaving the kingdom
had also been granted their own safe conduct, and the barons
of the Cinque Ports were told at the same time 'to secure them
a safe and speedy passage at moderate charges', an indication,
perhaps, of their community's impoverishment. The archbishop
of York had already taken steps to protect these Jews as they left
his jurisdiction.[57]

There is nothing to suggest that the Expulsion went other
than smoothly, certainly until the 2,000 or so departing Jews
reached the English coast. There are no reports of attacks or
massacres as the Jews travelled towards their ships. Once on
board, however, they were at the mercy of unscrupulous pirates.
One captain, presumably after having taken his fee for the passage, anchored in the Thames as the tide went out. Somehow
he persuaded his Jewish passengers to take a walk on the sands,

but he abandoned them and left them to drown as the tide rose again. The crew divided their property amongst themselves but were soon arrested and punished. Another incident took place near Burnham-on-Crouch in Essex, where a ship carrying Jewish passengers drifted ashore. All of them were robbed and murdered.[58] Other similar descriptions probably relate to the same events. And linked to them may also have been the release from Sandwich prison in July 1293 of Henry Adrian, 'who has been detained therein for two years for the death of Jews wherewith he is charged, and for other trespasses committed upon the Jews in their passage to parts beyond the sea'.[59] Such episodes were horrible but rare, it seems, in 1290. By the end of the year, a few Jews may have been prepared to run the risk of staying in England. But their numbers must have been tiny, and the only Jews who remained in England legally were those who had already converted to Christianity.

With the Jews gone, the winding-up of their affairs began. On 5 November 1290, after justifying the Expulsion on the basis of the Jews' persistent usury, the king cancelled the usurious elements of all outstanding Jewish loans, 'willing that nothing shall be exacted from the Christians except the principal debts that they received from the Jews'.[60] Meanwhile, orders had been issued to transport the *archae* from around the kingdom to London by 26 November, and chests from twenty-one separate towns and cities duly arrived.[61] Lists of the bonds in each *archa* were compiled, presumably with the intention at this stage of enforcing the debts now that they belonged to the king. Unfortunately, the lists have not survived for every *archa*; but the value of the bonds detailed on those lists which are still available is some £9,100. And the total value of all the bonds Edward I had collected by 1291 has been estimated at approximately £20,000.[62]

The king's officials were also given the task of dealing with the Jews' landed property. On 20 December 1290, Hugh of Kendall, a highly experienced royal servant, was appointed by the king 'to value and sell all the houses, rents and tenements which late belonged to the King's Jews'. Sheriffs were to receive the money from the eventual sales and account for it at the Exchequer.[63] In fact, the process of valuation had already begun before the date of Kendall's formal appointment; most of the sheriffs had been ordered to list and value Jewish houses at the same time as their colleagues had been ordered to arrange the transport of the *archae*, whilst some received separate instructions to do so in September.[64] Kendall's job appears to have been mostly a matter of supervising the process and making the final record of it. The lists he compiled contained details of Jewish properties sold off in sixteen different towns and cities.[65] Kendall's figures do not represent the value of all of the Jewish properties in England at the time of the Expulsion, however. Some, it should be remembered, were sold off by favoured Jews with royal permission just before the deadline for departure, and there were some disputes about whether certain properties had belonged to Jews or not. In the decade or so before 1290, too, the royal licences granting them permission to do so show that a significant number of English Jews must already have sold off many of their properties by the time the rest were confiscated. Nevertheless, Kendall's lists of former Jewish properties are certainly instructive. Most numerous and most valuable, not surprisingly, were those in London. Together they were worth more than half of the total value of all the Jewish properties sold after 1290.[66] Next on the list in terms of value, perhaps more surprisingly, were the Jewish properties of York. York's Jewish community was certainly in decline well before 1290, but its great houses, commented on by William of Newburgh in the twelfth century, may have survived as reminders of a more prosperous past.[67]

It has been calculated that 'between 1291 and 1292 the king made eighty-five separate grants which disposed of the property of 113 Jews'.[68] Naturally, some of his advisers and friends did well, as did some of their relatives and associates. Queen Eleanor's tailor was granted the synagogue in Canterbury, for example. And all of the Jewish property seized in Oxford, which was worth over £100 according to Kendall's account, was sold to William, the nephew of the king's chancellor, Robert Burnell. On the site which became known as 'Burnell's Inn', on the east side of St Aldate's where Christ Church now stands, William built a university *aula*, and on his death he left all his Oxford property to Balliol College.[69] The redistribution of Jewish property was not a free-for-all for royal favourites, however. Hugh of Kendall appears to have worked on the principle that he would secure the best price he could for any particular house or tenement. Former Jewish properties were redistributed 'among a wide range of social groups', although in York at least the most valuable were acquired by members of the local knightly class. By the end of 1290, Kendall had received nearly £700 from the sale proceeds of ex-Jewish property, and within six months of his appointment he had collected over £1,000. Ultimately, something over £1,800 was probably collected from the sale of former Jewish property.[70] Some of this money, just over £100, was spent on glazing windows at Westminster Abbey and on the decoration of Henry III's tomb there, thus making that monument 'an abiding memorial to the way in which Henry's son exploited his Jewish subjects after as well as before their ultimate departure from the kingdom'.[71]

The English Jewries were dissolved quickly and effectively in 1290–1 and with relatively little fuss. Not every ex-Jewish property was sold straight away, nor was every buyer prompt with his payments. Nevertheless, these were minor irritations, and by the spring of 1291 the bulk of the work had been done. As for King Edward, his attention must soon have turned to other things. On 28 November 1290, Queen Eleanor died at Harby in Lincolnshire, and by the time the king's period of mourning for his wife had ended, problems in Scotland had

probably begun to weigh heavily on his mind. In the late spring
and early summer of 1291, Edward was on the Scottish border
arbitrating between the rival claimants to the Scottish throne.
Consequently, Jewish affairs must once again have dropped down
the list of Edward's priorities. Perhaps this accounts in part for
his failure to collect the Jewish debts which had come into his
hands after the Expulsion. It has been estimated that by 1291 the
bonds Edward's agents had collected from the provincial *archae*
had a face value of some £20,000.[72] However, there is nothing
to suggest that the government made a systematic attempt to call
them in. The receipts of the Exchequer of the Jews for the years
immediately after the Expulsion were insignificant. In the year
from November 1290 only £195 was received, and in the four
subsequent years (after which separate accounts were no longer
kept) the average amount received was only just over £88.[73]
Why Edward was prepared to forego such a potentially lucrative
source of funds is unclear, especially when, immediately after
the Expulsion, all the indications were that he was planning to
collect what he was now owed. His later reluctance to enforce
payment of these debts certainly seems like a deliberate change
of royal policy. Debts owed to the king, or more particularly the
promise of their relaxation and the threat of their enforcement,
had long been used by English rulers as tools of both patronage
and political control. Perhaps Edward decided to tread softly
with the debtors in the hope of securing their support in the
future. Or perhaps this easy-going royal attitude towards Jewish
debts formed part of the understanding reached between the
king and the Commons after the parliamentary negotiations of
July 1290. It is going too far, however, to suggest that 'financial
profit on Edward's behalf is also unlikely to have been a prime
motive for the Expulsion, not least because he never claimed the
Jews' debts'. As has been seen, Edward received over £100,000
in taxation because he had agreed to expel the Jews.[74]

7

Aftermath

In 1356, in the *Domus Conversorum* in London, Claricia of Exeter, 'the last survivor on English soil of the pre-expulsion Jewish community', died. The convert daughter of Jacob Copin, she had first been admitted to the *Domus* some time before 1280. During the early years of the fourteenth century, however, she had left the comparative safety of the community to live in Exeter, where she had married and had children. But in 1330 she returned to the *Domus*, and appears to have remained there for the rest of her life.[1] The worlds of Claricia's youth and old age must have been very different ones. As a girl, she would have been part of a struggling yet still viable Jewish community; by the time she died, that community was little more than a distant memory. She may have spent some of her time in the *Domus* with other converts who remembered the years before 1290, but there can never have been many of these. In 1290, there were about 100 residents housed there, men and women, and although the *Domus* continued in use for the rest of the Middle Ages, its numbers never reached this level again.[2] After the Expulsion, it did not take long before what remained of the post-conquest Jewish presence in England was made up mostly of reminiscences and myths.

There were other memorials, too, of course. Several of England's older cities still have streets or areas named after their previous inhabitants, Jewbury in York, for example, or Old Jewry in London. One or two of the great stone houses built by the Jews of twelfth-century Lincoln remain standing even today, and for a considerable time after 1290 it is likely that the physical reminders of medieval English Jewry, the other great houses in York, London and elsewhere, the synagogues and the cemeteries, for example, remained in place. There were no English Jews to live, pray or be buried in them, however. Some converts, like Claricia, remained, and from time to time, other Jews appear to have visited England from the continent. In 1309, one Master Elias was given a safe conduct to enter England; it has been suggested that he came in an attempt to persuade Edward II to readmit Jews to England.[3] If this was his aim, he was, of course, unsuccessful (they were not allowed to return until 1656), and thereafter there is only the occasional reference to Jews in England for much of the rest of the medieval period.

As for what happened to the English exiles of 1290, little is known for certain. Many would probably have fled in the first instance to France. However, on 16 February 1291, Philip IV ordered the expulsion of Jews newly arrived from across the Channel. Nevertheless, some still remained in France and were paying taxes in Paris in 1292, 1296 and 1297. Bonamy, the last of the great Jewish financiers of York (he was, indeed, 'the final English Jewish moneylender of substance'), was in Paris in 1292 and continuing to do business with the archbishop of York.[4] He was a special case, however, as the royal protection he had secured during his departure from England had showed. If Bonamy stayed in France thereafter, though, and if he was still alive in 1306, even he would have been hard pressed to survive the general expulsion enacted in that year by Philip IV, which was 'by far the most significant suffered by medieval Ashkenazic Jewry to date'.[5] His co-religionists from England probably fared less well more quickly after 1290 and were scattered across Europe and beyond. It has been suggested that some may have ended up in other parts of the British Isles; others as far away as Egypt and the Mediterranean.[6]

Fairly quickly then, it seems, with little disturbance to the general flow of events and with little impact on the contemporary imagination, English medieval Jewry had ceased to exist. But the suddenness of its end and the lack of contemporary reaction to its extermination should not obscure the significance of its history. Over the 200 years or so before 1290, Jewish communities had grown and spread across England. Albeit with difficulties, they had prospered in the twelfth century, and, even during the thirteenth century when they were much more on the defensive and subject to vicious hostility and officially sanctioned persecution, they had continued to show their enterprise, resilience and adaptability. Medieval English Jewry never achieved the cultural and religious creativity of its northern French cousin, but it was only at the height of its financial, commercial and political power for a little over a century between the 1140s and the 1240s, and even within that period there were serious setbacks, in 1190 and 1210 for example. Given the amount of time they had and the circumstances within which they lived and worked, the achievements of England's medieval Jews were considerable.

By contrast, the role played in this history by the English Jews' Christian hosts is worthy of anything but praise. Of course there would have been Christians who treated Jews relatively well and others who were indifferent to them. But growing popular antagonism towards the Jews combined with pressing royal financial needs, the increasingly inflexible and dogmatic position of the Church and the Jews' own vulnerability in the face of such developments meant that, in the end, coexistence became steadily more difficult. It was also in England between 1066 and 1290 that a powerful, tenacious and ultimately disastrous legacy of anti-Jewish feeling originated. The massacres of 1189–90 and the executions of 1278–9 were as bad as anything of their kind in medieval Europe; but it was the death of William of Norwich in 1144 that gave rise to the myth of Jewish ritual murder, a belief of such pernicious strength that its influence continued to be felt even during the horrors of the twentieth century. And the Expulsion of 1290, so comprehensive, decisive and effective, became the model for later acts of the same kind. Philip IV's edict of 1306 built on the precedent it set, as did rulers across Europe in subsequent generations. In terms of time and numbers, therefore, the story of England's medieval Jews plays only a relatively small part in the wider history of Ashkenazic Jewry. 'Nevertheless', in Cecil Roth's words, 'England had played an important and unenviable role in the martyrdom of the Jewish people'.[7]

The Counties and Principal Towns of England, *c.*1200

Notes

Introduction

1   Colin Richmond, 'Englishness and Medieval Anglo-Jewry', in *The Jewish Heritage in British History: Englishness and Jewishness*, ed. Tony Kushner (London, 1992), pp.42–59.
2   Genesis, 12:1–3.

1: The Jews in Anglo-Norman England, 1066–1154

1   Robert Chazan, *Church, State and Jew in the Middle Ages* (West Orange, N.J., 1980), pp.99–100.
2   Idem., '1007–1012: Initial Crisis for North-European Jewry', *Proceedings of the American Academy for Jewish Research*, 38–9 (1970–71), pp.101–18.
3   Simon Keynes on 'Jews' in *The Blackwell Encyclopaedia of Anglo-Saxon England*, ed. Michael Lapidge, John Blair, Simon Keynes and Donald Scragg (Oxford, 1999), p.262; J. Campbell, 'The Late Anglo-Saxon State: a Maximum View', *Proceedings of the British Academy*, 87 (1994), pp.61–2, repr. in idem., *The Anglo-Saxon State* (London, 2000), p.26.
4   Robert C. Stacey, 'Anti-Semitism and the medieval English state', in *The Medieval State: Essays Presented to James Campbell*, ed. J.R. Maddicott and D.M. Palliser (London, 2000), pp.163–77, at p.166.
5   William of Malmesbury, *Gesta Regum Anglorum*, ed. and trans. R.A.B. Mynors; completed by R.M. Thomson and M. Winterbottom, 2 vols (Oxford and New York, 1998), i p.563.
6   Robert C. Stacey, 'Jewish lending and the medieval English economy', in *A Commercialising Economy. England, 1086 to c.1300*, ed. R.H. Britnell and B.M.S. Campbell (Manchester, 1995), pp.78–101, at pp.78–82.

7   On this subject generally, see Robert Bartlett, *The Making of Europe* (London, 1993).

8   For a discussion of the amount of money which may have been in circulation in about 1066, see Nicholas Mayhew, 'Modelling medieval monetisation', in *A commercialising economy. England 1086 to c.1300*, ed. Britnell and Campbell, pp.55–77, esp. at pp.62–8.

9   Robert Chazan, *European Jewry and the First Crusade* (London, 1987), pp.19–20; idem, *Church, State and Jew in the Middle Ages*, pp.57–9.

10 William of Malmesbury, *Gesta Regum*, i p.563; Joe Hillaby, 'Jewish Colonisation in the Twelfth Century', in *Jews in Medieval Britain. Historical, Literary and Archaeological Perspectives*, ed. Patricia Skinner (Woodbridge, 2003), pp.15–40, at pp.16–17. For the events at Rouen, see the account by Guibert of Nogent in *Self and Society in Medieval France*, ed. J. Benton (New York, 1970), pp.134–5.

11 Joe Hillaby, 'The London Jewry: William I to John', *TJHSE*, 33 (1992–1994), pp.1–44, at pp.4–7; Cecil Roth, *History of the Jews in England* (3rd edn, Oxford, 1964), p.7; H.G. Richardson, *The English Jewry under Angevin Kings* (London, 1960), pp.6–8.

12 *PR 31 Henry I*, pp.149; Robert Bartlett, *England under the Norman and Angevin Kings, 1075–1225* (Oxford, 2000), p.213.

13 C.W. Hollister, *Henry I* (Yale, 2001), p.2; J. Green, *The Government of England under Henry I* (Cambridge, 1986), p.162.

14 Hillaby, 'The London Jewry: William I to John', p.12.

15 *PR 31 Henry I*, pp.53, 149.

16 Ibid., p.148.

17 Stacey, 'Jewish lending and the medieval English economy', p.83.

18 *PR 31 Henry I*, p.149.

19 Stacey, 'Jewish lending and the medieval English economy', pp.83–5; Hillaby, 'Jewish Colonisation', p.19.

20 Hillaby, 'The London Jewry: William I to John', p.8; Richardson, *English Jewry under Angevin Kings*, pp.111 n.5, 156.

21 *Jocelin of Brakelond. Chronicle of the Abbey of Bury St Edmunds*, trans. Diana Greenway and Jane Sayers (Oxford, 1989), p.10.

22 Robin R. Mundill, *England's Jewish Solution. Experiment and Expulsion, 1262-1290* (Cambridge, 1998), p.18.

23 Ibid., p.130 for these and other examples.

24 Bruce R. O'Brien, *God's Peace and King's Peace: the Laws of Edward the Confessor* (Philadelphia, 1999), p.185.

25 *Rot. Chart.*, I i pp.93–93b; *Foedera*, I i p.51. An English translation of John's charter is included in Chazan, *Church, State and Jew in the Middle Ages*, pp.77–9.

26 For one recent description of these events, see T. Asbridge, *The First Crusade. A New History* (London, 2004), pp.84–8.

27 For a suggestion that seigneurial Jewries might have been established under Henry I, see K.T. Streit, 'The expansion of the Jewish community in the reign of King Stephen', *Albion*, 25 (1993), pp.177–92, at pp.178–9.

28 For a different view, namely that Stephen actively encouraged the expansion of provincial Jewries during his reign, and that their growth was more a sign of his political strength than his political weakness, see ibid.

29 Stacey, 'Jewish lending and the medieval English economy', p.85; Richardson, *English Jewry under Angevin Kings*, p.9; Bartlett, *England under the Norman and Angevin Kings*, p.349.

30 Hillaby, 'Jewish Colonisation', pp.22, 24; Stacey, 'Jewish lending and the medieval English economy', p.86 n.36.

31 Richardson, *English Jewry under Angevin Kings*, 12–13; Hillaby, 'The London Jewry:

William I to John', pp.14–15; idem., 'Jewish Colonisation', p.25.

32 Chazan, *European Jewry and the First Crusade*, pp.169–79; *The Jews and the Crusaders. The Hebrew Chronicles of the First and Second Crusades*, trans. and ed. Shlomo Eidelberg (Madison, 1977), p.131; Roth, *History of the Jews*, p.10.

33 *EHD* II, p.212.

34 The best treatment of this episode is still Gavin I. Langmuir, 'Thomas of Monmouth: Detector of Ritual Murder', *Speculum*, 59 (1984), pp.820-846. But for a more recent re-examination of Thomas of Monmouth's role in the creation of the ritual murder myth, see John McCulloh, 'Jewish ritual murder: William of Norwich, Thomas of Monmouth and the early dissemination of the myth', *Speculum*, 72 (1997), pp.698–740.

35 For the controversial view that the blood libel may be of older, continental origin, see Israel Jacob Yuval, '"Vengeance and damnation, blood and defamation": from Jewish martyrdom to blood libel accusations', *Zion*, 58 (1993), pp.33–90.

36 Langmuir, 'Thomas of Monmouth', p.844; Richmond, 'Englishness and Medieval Anglo-Jewry', p.54.

37 This episode in described in A. Jessopp and M.R. James, *The Life and Miracles of St. William of Norwich, by Thomas of Monmouth* (Cambridge, 1896), pp.43–8, 92–3, 99–110. Much of it is usefully contained too in *English Lawsuits from William I to Richard I*, ed. R.C. Van Caenegem, 2 vols (Selden Society, 1990–91), i no.321.

38 Bartlett, *England under the Norman and Angevin Kings*, p.168.

39 Roth, *History of the Jews*, pp.7–8; idem., *The Jews of Medieval Oxford* (Oxford Historical Society, new series, 9, 1945–6), pp.2–3.

2: The Jews in Angevin England, 1154–1216

1 *Materials for the History of Thomas Becket, Archbishop of Canterbury*, ed. J.C. Robertson, 7 vols (RS, 1875–85), iii p.19.

2 Stacey, 'Jewish lending and the medieval English economy', pp.85–6, esp. n.35; Hillaby, 'The London Jewry: William I to John', pp.14–15.

3 Stacey, 'Jewish lending and the medieval English economy', p.86 n.35.

4 See above, pp.31, 57 and n.6.

5 *Rot. Chart.*, I i pp.93–93b; *Foedera*, I i p.51.

6 *Chronicles of the Reigns of Stephen, Henry I and Richard I*, ed. R. Howlett, 4 vols (RS, 1885–90), i p.280.

7 For what follows in this paragraph, see Richardson, *English Jewry under Angevin Kings*, pp.51–5; H. Jenkinson, 'William Cade, a financier of the twelfth century', *EHR*, 28 (1913), pp.209–27; *ODNB* on 'Cade, William'.

8 Richardson, *English Jewry under Angevin Kings*, p.53.

9 *Dialogus de Scaccario and Constitutio Domus Regis*, ed. C. Johnson (revised edn, Oxford, 1983), p.99; *Tractatus de legibus et consuetudines regni Anglie qui Glanvilla vocatur*, ed. G.D.G. Hall (Oxford, 1965), p.89.

10 Richardson, *English Jewry under Angevin Kings*, pp.68, 247–53; Bartlett, *England under the Norman and Angevin Kings*, p.351; *ODNB* on 'Lincoln, Aaron of'.

11 Richardson, *English Jewry under Angevin Kings*, pp.60–3; Hillaby, 'The London Jewry: William I to John', p.21.

12 Richardson, *English Jewry under Angevin Kings*, p.63.

13 *The Historical Works of Gervase of Canterbury*, ed. W. Stubbs, 2 vols (RS, 1879–80), i p.422.

14 Richardson, *English Jewry under Angevin Kings*, pp.162–3; Hillaby, 'The London Jewry: William I to John', pp.21–4.

15 Hillaby, 'Jewish Colonisation', p.29; Roth, *History of the Jews*, p.17.

16 Roth, *History of the Jews*, p.13. For Gloucester, see J. Hillaby, 'The ritual child murder accusation: its dissemination and Harold of Gloucester', *JHS*, 34 (1994–6), pp.69–109. There is a list of all the main ritual murder allegations at ibid., p.86. For Bury St. Edmunds, see *Jocelin of Brakelond*, pp.xxx, 15, 128.
17 For this episode, see R. Chazan, *Medieval Jewry in Northern France* (Baltimore, 1973), pp.64–70, 74–6; idem., *Church, State and Jew in the Middle Ages*, pp.310–12.
18 Mundill, *England's Jewish Solution*, p.51.
19 Matthew Paris, *Historia Anglorum*, ed. F. Madden, 3 vols (RS, 1866–9), ii p.9.
20 Chazan, *Church, State and Jew in the Middle Ages*, pp.158–61.
21 Ibid., p.161.
22 *Chronicles of the Reigns of Stephen, Henry I and Richard I*, i p.299.
23 R.B. Dobson, *The Jews of Medieval York and the Massacre of March 1190* (Borthwick Papers, no.45, York, 1974), p.25 n.81; Hillaby, 'Jewish Colonisation, pp.30–1.
24 Roth, *History of the Jews*, pp.24–5; *Jocelin of Brakelond*, pp.41–2.
25 For the best analysis of the York massacre, and for most of what follows on it here, see Dobson, *The Jews of Medieval York*. The fullest contemporary account is by William of Newburgh in *Chronicles of the Reigns of Stephen, Henry I and Richard I*, i pp.312–22.
26 Ibid., pp.312–13, 314.
27 Ibid., pp.313–14, 316.
28 D.A. Carpenter, *The Struggle for Mastery. Britain, 1066-1284* (London, 2003), p.250.
29 Richardson, *English Jewry under Angevin Kings*, p.136; Roth, *History of the Jews*, pp.28–31; Paul Brand, 'The Jewish Community in the Records of Royal Government', in *Jews in Medieval Britain*, ed. Skinner, pp.73–83, at pp.73–9.
30 *EHD* III, pp.303, 305–6.
31 Dobson, *The Jews of Medieval York*, p.30.
32 Richmond, 'Englishness and Medieval Anglo-Jewry', p.51.
33 Richardson, *English Jewry under Angevin Kings*, pp.164–5.
34 For this and what follows on the Northampton *donum*, see I. Abrahams, 'The Northampton "Donum" of 1194', *TJHSE*, Miscellanies, I (1925), pp.lix–lxxiv; Hillaby, 'Jewish Colonisation', pp.32–4.
35 Above, pp.31, 41.
36 *Rot. Litt. Pat.*, p.33
37 Carpenter, *Struggle for Mastery*, p.270.
38 On this subject more generally, see J.C. Holt, *The Northerners* (Oxford, 1961), pp.143–74; N. Barratt, 'The Revenue of King John', *EHR*, III (1996), pp.835–55.
39 *Rot. Oblat.*, pp.391, 402–3, 418; *Rot. Litt. Claus.*, i pp.112b–113; *Rot. Litt. Pat.*, pp.81b–82.
40 *Ann. Waverley*, p.264. For most of what follows here on the 1210 tallage, see Richardson, *English Jewry under Angevin Kings*, pp.167–72.
41 Robert C. Stacey, 'The English Jews under Henry III', in *Jews in Medieval Britain*, ed. Skinner, pp.41–54, at p.43.
42 *Oxenedes*, p.125.
43 Matthew Paris, *Chronica Majora*, ed. H.R. Luard, 7 vols (RS, London, 1872-84), ii p.528.
44 Richardson, *English Jewry under Angevin Kings*, p.167; Roth, *History of the Jews*, p.35.
45 Mundill, *England's Jewish Solution*, p.55.
46 *Excerpta e Rotulis Finium in Turri Londiniensi Asservatis ... AD 1216-72*, ed. C. Roberts, 2 vols (Record Commission, 1835-6), i pp.412, 418–19.
47 For what follows, see Holt, *The Northerners*, pp.164–74.
48 Idem., *Magna Carta* (2nd edn, Cambridge, 1992), p.211.
49 *Radulphi de Coggeshall Chronicon Anglicanum*, ed. J. Stevenson (RS, 1875), p.171.
50 *EHD* III, p.318.
51 Holt, *Magna Carta*, pp.335–6.

3: Jewish Life and Lending in the Twelfth and Thirteenth Centuries

1 B. Lionel Abrahams, 'The Condition of the Jews at the Time of their Expulsion in 1290', *TJHSE*, 2 (1894–5), p.79.

2 *Oxenedes*, p.277; *Flores Historiarum*, ed. H.R. Luard, 3 vols (RS, 1890), iii p.70.

3 Roth, *History of the Jews*, p.276; V.D. Lipman, 'Anatomy of Medieval Anglo-Jewry', *TJHSE* 21 (1968), pp.64–5. For discussions of overall population figures, see R.H. Britnell, *Britain and Ireland 1050–1530. Economy and Society* (Oxford, 2004), pp.80–2; Mayhew, 'Modelling medieval monetisation', pp.57–9.

4 Abrahams, 'The Northampton "Donum" of 1194', pp.lix–lxxiv; Hillaby, 'Jewish Colonisation', p.15.

5 Above, pp.39–40.

6 For a discussion of this, see Mundill, *England's Jewish Solution*, pp.21–5.

7 Lipman, 'Anatomy of Medieval English Jewry', p.68; Barrie Dobson, 'The role of Jewish Women in Medieval England', in *Christianity and Judaism* (*Studies in Church History*, 29, Oxford, 1992), pp.145–68, at pp.150–1. According to Stacey, with the exception of London, 'the Jewish communities of England probably contained only between 50 and 300 persons each': 'The Conversion of Jews to Christianity in thirteenth-century England', *Speculum*, 67 (1992), pp.263–83 at p.279.

8 *Gerald of Wales. The Journey through Wales and the Description of Wales*, trans. Lewis Thorpe (London, 1978), p.204.

9 *Close Rolls*, 1234–7, p.425; *Liber*, p.237.

10 Above, p.55.

11 Cecil Roth, 'A day in the life of a medieval English Jew', in idem., *Essays and Portraits in Anglo-Jewish History* (London and Philadelphia, 1962), pp.26–45, at pp.34–5.

12 *Jocelin of Brakelond*, p.10.

13 Jane McComish, 'The Medieval Jewish Cemetery at Jewbury, York', *Jewish Culture and History*, vol. 3 no 2 (Winter, 2000), pp.21–30; Roth, 'A day in the life', p.27.

14 Mundill, *England's Jewish Solution*, p.51.

15 See plates 2, 7.

16 Paul Hyams, 'The Jewish Minority in Medieval England, 1066–1290', *JJS*, 25 (1974), pp.270–93, at p.274.

17 See above, pp.135–6.

18 Bartlett, *England under the Norman and Angevin Kings*, p.356.

19 *The Chronicle of Bury St. Edmunds, 1212-1301*, ed. A. Gransden (London, 1964), p.58; Roth, *History of the Jews*, p.83; Mundill, *England's Jewish Solution*, p.48; Hyams, 'The Jewish Minority', p.275.

20 Above, p.27.

21 J. Hillaby, 'Beth Miqdash Me-at: the synagogues of medieval England', *Journal of Ecclesiastical History*, 44 (1991), p.194.

22 Ibid., p.183.

23 Mundill, *England's Jewish Solution*, p.32.

24 Hyams, 'Jewish Minority', p.286; Roth, 'A day in the life', pp.28–30.

25 Mundill, *England's Jewish Solution*, p.28; Roth, *History of the Jews*, p.93.

26 Idem., 'Why Anglo-Jewish history?' *TJHSE*, xxii (1968–9), p.27. For a general survey of the intellectual achievements of medieval Anglo-Jewry, see idem., *History of the Jews*, pp.124–9. For Norwich, see Vivian D. Lipman, *The Jews of Medieval Norwich* (London, 1967), ch.VIII.

27 Bartlett, *England under the Norman and Angevin Kings*, p.348; Lipman, 'Anatomy', p.69; Dobson, 'The role of Jewish women', pp.152–3; Hillaby, 'Jewish

Colonisation', p.35.

28 Suzanne Bartlet, 'Women in the Medieval Anglo-Jewish Community', in *Jews in Medieval Britain*, ed. Skinner, pp.113–27, at pp.115, 122.

29 Dobson, 'The role of Jewish women', p.154.

30 Suzanne Bartlet, 'Three Jewish Businesswomen in Thirteenth-Century Winchester', *Jewish Culture and History*, vol 3 no 2 (Winter, 2000), pp.31–54 at p.31.

31 Bartlet, 'Women in the Medieval Anglo-Jewish Community', pp.119–24; Dobson, 'The role of Jewish women', pp.154–8.

32 Above, p.66.

33 Bartlet, 'Three Jewish Businesswomen', *passim*; quotation at p.47; Dobson, 'The role of Jewish women', p.154. Also on Licoricia and David of Oxford, see R. Berman Brown and S. McCartney, 'David of Oxford and Licoricia of Winchester: glimpses into a Jewish family in thirteenth-century England', *JHS*, 39 (2004), pp.1–34; Roth, *The Jews of Medieval Oxford*, pp.46–57.

34 Dobson, 'The role of Jewish women', p.146.

35 Roth, 'A day in the life', p.32.

36 See M.B. Honeybourne, 'The pre-expulsion cemetery of the Jews in London', *TJHSE* 20 (1959–61), pp.145–59.

37 Bartlett, *England under the Norman and Angevin Kings*, p.348.

38 *The Chronicles of the Reigns of Henry II and Richard I, A.D.1169-92*, ed. William Stubbs, 2 vols (RS, 1867), i p.182; *Chronica Magistri Rogeri de Hovedene*, ed. William Stubbs, 4 vols (RS, 1868–71), ii p.137.

39 For these and other example, see Richardson, *English Jewry under Angevin Kings*, pp.26–7; Roth, *History of the Jews*, pp.102, 113–14. For John's use of Jews as crossbowmen, see also Stacey, 'The Conversion of Jews', p.266 n.19.

40 *Rot. Litt. Claus.*, i p.220.

41 Hyams, 'Jewish Minority', p.273.

42 Richmond, 'Englishness and Medieval Anglo-Jewry', p.53.

43 Stacey, 'Jewish lending and the medieval English economy', p.97.

44 Ibid., p.94.

45 Roth, 'A day in the life', p.36.

46 Lipman, *The Jews of Medieval Norwich*, p.48.

47 Mundill, *England's Jewish Solution*, p.111.

48 For more on what follows, see ibid., pp.111–13.

49 *Rot. Chart.*, p.93; *EHD* III, p.350.

50 *EHD* II, p.450.

51 Dobson, 'The role of Jewish women', p.156; *Jocelin of Brakelond*, pp.3–4.

52 *EHD* III, p.350.

53 Stacey, 'Jewish lending and the medieval English economy', p.96.

54 Joe Hillaby, 'A magnate among the marchers: Hamo of Hereford, his family and his clients, 1218–1253', *JHS* 31 (1988-90), pp.23–82.

55 Lipman, *The Jews of Medieval Norwich*, pp.93–4.

56 Peter Elman, 'The economic causes of the expulsion of the Jews in 1290', *Economic History Review*, 7 (1936–7), pp.145–54, at p.148.

57 Richardson, *English Jewry under Angevin Kings*, pp.89–100.

58 R.B. Dobson, 'The Decline and Expulsion of the Medieval Jews of York', *TJHSE* (1979), pp.34–52, at pp.39–40.

59 Hillaby, 'Jewish Colonisation', p.33.

60 Richardson, *English Jewry under Angevin Kings*, p.99.

61 *Jocelin of Brakelond*, pp.3–4, 6–7, 29.

4: *King Henry III and the Assault on England's Jews*

1 For a much fuller description of the events of 1216–17, see D.A. Carpenter, *The Minority of Henry III* (London, 1990), ch.2.
2 For more on what follows, see Richardson, *English Jewry under Angevin Kings*, pp.178–83; Roth, *History of the Jews*, 39–41; Carpenter, *Minority of Henry III*, 82–3.
3 Hillaby, 'Jewish Colonisation', p.28.
4 *Rot. Litt. Claus.*, i pp.354b, 357, 359b.
5 Roth, *History of the Jews*, p.41; *Royal and other Historical Letters illustrative of the Reign of Henry III*, ed. W.W. Shirley, 2 vols (RS, London, 1862-6), i pp.35–6; *ODNB* on 'Norwich, Isaac of'.
6 *Rot. Litt. Claus.*, i p.378b.
7 Richardson, *English Jewry under Angevin Kings*, pp.179–80; Nicholas Vincent, 'Two papal letters on the wearing of the Jewish badge, 1221 and 1239', *JHS*, 34 (1994–6), pp.209–24.
8 Dobson, 'Decline and Expulsion', p.36.
9 *CPR 1261–25*, pp.180–1
10 Robert C. Stacey, *Politics, Policy and Finance under Henry III* (Oxford, 1987), pp.143–4.
11 Chazan, *Medieval Jewry in Northern France*, pp.104–13; quotation at p.112; idem., *Church, State and Jew in the Middle Ages*, pp.213–16, 283–4.
12 Mundill, *England's Jewish Solution*, p.265. For Montfort and Leicester, see J.R. Maddicott, *Simon de Montfort* (London, 1994), p.15.
13 The best treatment of the subject of Jewish conversion to Christianity is Stacey, 'The Conversion of the Jews'.
14 Ibid., p.270.
15 *Cal.Ch.R. 1226-57*, p.143; *Foedera*, I i p.201. For more on the *Domus*, see M. Adler, *The Jews of Medieval England* (London, 1939), pp.279–339; Stacey, 'Conversion of the Jews', pp.273–5. For Henry III's piety, see Carpenter, *Struggle for Mastery*, pp.338–9.
16 Stacey, *Politics, Policy and Finance*, p.145.
17 *Curia Regis Rolls of the Reign of Henry III*, 15, 1233–7 (London, 1972), no.1320; Rigg, *Select Pleas*, pp.xliv-xlvii; Matthew Paris, *Chronica Majora*, iv pp.30–1; *Close Rolls 1234–7*, p.17; *Close Rolls 1237–42*, pp.168, 175, 247; Roth, *History of the Jews*, pp.53-4. The rest of this paragraph is based on Stacey's analysis: *Politics, Policy and Finance*, pp.145–59.
18 Dobson, 'Decline and Expulsion', p.36.
19 For Aaron, see *ODNB* on 'York, Aaron of'; Dobson, 'Decline and Expulsion', pp.35–7.
20 Stacey, 'The English Jews under Henry III', p.46.
21 Dobson, 'Decline and Expulsion', p.36.
22 See above, p.60.
23 Dobson, 'Decline and Expulsion', p.36; *Close Rolls, 1254-6*, p.140; Matthew Paris, *Chronica Majora*, v p.136.
24 Stacey, *Politics, Policy and Finance*, p.154.
25 Idem., 'Jewish lending and the medieval English economy', pp.94–5.
26 Idem., 'The English Jews under Henry III', p.41.
27 Carpenter, *Struggle for Mastery*, p.401; *The Early Rolls of Merton College*, ed. J.R.L. Highfield (Oxford Historical Society, new series, 18, 1964), pp.12–13, 17, 34–6.
28 Matthew Paris, *Chronica Majora*, v 114–15.
29 N. Denholm-Young, *Richard of Cornwall* (Oxford, 1947), p.70; Mundill, *England's Jewish Solution*, pp.60–1.

30 Margaret Howell, *Eleanor of Provence* (Oxford, 1998), pp.278–9.

31 *Documents of the Baronial Movement of Reform and Rebellion, 1258–67*, ed. R.F.
    Treharne and I.J. Sanders (Oxford, 1973), p.87.

32 Dobson, 'Decline and Expulsion', p.39. For the most recent synthesis and
    discussion of the debate on 'the crisis of the knightly class', see Peter Coss, *The
    Origins of the English Gentry* (Cambridge, 2003), esp. Chapter 4.

33 Joe Hillaby, 'The Hereford Jewry 1179–1290 – Aaron le Blund and the last
    decades of Hereford Jewry 1253–1290', *Transactions of the Woolhope Naturalists Field
    Club*, 46(3) (1990), pp.432–87; above, p.91.

34 Dobson, 'Decline and Expulsion', p.39.

35 Hyams, 'Jewish Minority', p.291.

36 For Elias' career, see *ODNB* on 'Eveske, Elias l''; Joe Hillaby, 'London: the 13th-
    century Jewry Revisited', *TJHSE*, 32 (1990–92), pp.89–158, at pp.130–4. Howell
    discusses some of the favours secured for the Eveske family by the Queen: *Eleanor
    of Provence*, p.277.

37 W.C. Jordan, Louis IX and the Challenge of the Crusade (Princeton, 1979),
    pp.154–5; Chazan, Medieval Jewry in Northern France, p.121.

38 *Close Rolls 1251–3*, pp.312–13; Rigg, *Select Pleas*, p.xlix.

39 Mundill, *England's Jewish Solution*, p.58; Robert C. Stacey, '1240–60: a Watershed
    in Anglo-Jewish Relations?', *Bulletin of the Institute of Historical Research*, 61 (1988),
    pp.135–50, at pp.146–7; *Close Rolls 1251-3*, pp.312–13.

40 Stacey, 'Watershed', pp.139–40; Matthew Paris, *Chronica Majora*, v p.441.

41 Ibid., iv pp.377–8.

42 The best treatment of these events is Gavin I. Langmuir, 'The Knight's Tale of
    Young Hugh of Lincoln', *Speculum*, 47 (1972), pp.459–82. Unless stated otherwise,
    the details of the story used here are derived from Langmuir's reconstruction.

43 For John of Lexinton, see ibid., pp. 469–82, and *ODNB* on 'Lexinton, John of'.

44 Dobson, 'Decline and Expulsion', p.36.

45 For more on what follows in this paragraph, see Carpenter, *Struggle for Mastery*,
    pp.340–361.

46 *Liber*, pp.50–1.

47 *Ann. Dunstable*, p.230.

48 *Wykes*, 141–3.

49 400: *Wykes*, p.142; more than 500: *Liber*, p.62.

50 *Liber*, p.62.

51 *Ann. Dunstable*, p.230; Roth, *History of the Jews*, p.62.

52 For the Leicester expulsion, see above, pp.86, 147. The comment about Montfort
    is from F.M. Powicke, *King Henry III and the Lord Edward*, 2 vols (Oxford, 1947), ii
    p.447. For Montfort's piety more generally, see Maddicott, *Simon de Montfort*, ch.3
    and *passim*.

53 *CPR 1258–66*, p.628; Rigg, *Select Pleas*, p.44.

54 Stacey, 'The English Jews under Henry III', p.53.

55 Carpenter, *Struggle for Mastery*, p.375. What follows here is based on Carpenter's
    analysis: ibid., pp.375–6.

56 Ibid., p.376.

57 *CPR 1258–66*, pp.323, 420–1, 431, 577.

58 *Liber*, 74.

59 For Deyville, see *ODNB* on 'Deyville, Sir John de'

60 *The Chronicle of Walter of Guisborough*, ed. H. Rothwell (Camden Society, 1957),
    p.203; *Nicholai Triveti Annales*, ed. T. Hog (London, 1845), p.271. I am grateful to
    David Carpenter for providing me with these references.

61 *CPR 1266–72*, pp.13, 24, 29.

62 *CPR 1266–72*, p.628.

63 *CPR 1266–72*, p.345; *Close Rolls 1268–72*, pp.53–4; *Medieval English Jews and Royal Officials: Entries of Jewish Interest in the English Memoranda Rolls, 1266–1293*, ed. Zefira Entin Rokeah (Jerusalem, 2000), no.181.
64 *CPR 1266–72*, pp.545–6.
65 *Close Rolls 1268–72*, p.116.
66 Rigg, *Select Pleas*, pp.xlix–li; *CPR 1266–72*, p.376.
67 Denholm-Young, *Richard of Cornwall*, p.143.
68 Richardson, *English Jewry under Angevin Kings*, pp.73, 104–5.
69 Above, pp.115–17
70 *CPR 1266–72*, p.598; *Foedera*, I i, p.489; Rigg, *Select Pleas*, pp.l–lv; Roth, *History of the Jews*, pp.65–6.
71 *Medieval English Jews*, ed. Rokeah, no.449; *CPREJ*, ii p.103.
72 Chazan, *Medieval Jewry in Northern France*, p.153.

5: *King Edward I and the Jews*

1 Michael Prestwich, *Edward I* (Yale, 1997), pp.9–11.
2 *CPR 1258-66*, pp.233, 263, 283; Prestwich, *Edward I*, p.38.
3 For two analyses of the Oxford incident, see C. Cluse, 'Stories of breaking and taking the cross: a possible context for the Oxford incident of 1268', *Revue d'histoire ecclésiastique*, 90 (1995), pp.396–442, and Roth, *The Jews of Medieval Oxford*, pp.151–4.
4 Chazan, *Medieval Jewry in Northern France*, pp.148–51.
5 Rigg, *Select Pleas*, p.xlix.
6 For most of what follows here, see J.R. Maddicott, 'The Crusade Taxation of 1268–70 and the Development of Parliament', *TCE* II, pp.93–117. For the content of the Provisions of the Jewry, see above, pp.109–10.
7 Maddicott, 'Crusade Taxation', p.102.
8 *Close Rolls 1268–72*, p.268.
9 Maddicott, 'Crusade Taxation', p.110; Robert C. Stacey, 'Parliamentary negotiation and the Expulsion of the Jews from England', *TCE* VI, pp. 77–101, at p.95.
10 *CPR 1272–81*, p.76.
11 Prestwich, *Edward I*, pp.91–101.
12 Stacey, 'Parliamentary negotiation', p.97.
13 Paul Brand, 'Jews and the Law in England, 1275–90', *EHR*, 115 (2000), pp.1138–58, at p.1140.
14 I have used the text of the statute found in *EHD* III, pp.411–12.
15 Above, p.95–6.
16 Roth, *History of the Jews*, p.71.
17 Mundill, *England's Jewish Solution*, p.120.
18 Brand, 'Jews and the Law', p.1153.
19 *EHD* III, pp.412–13.
20 Mundill, *England's Jewish Solution*, pp.124–145.
21 Ibid., pp.78–91.
22 Stacey, 'The English Jews under Henry III', pp.49–50; Mundill, *England's Jewish Solution*, p.90; above, pp.88–90.
23 *Wykes*, p.278.
24 'That the London Jewry was a centre of this traffic, in which Christians participated, there is no manner of doubt': Richardson, *English Jewry under Angevin Kings*, p.217.
25 *CPR 1272-81*, p.236.
26 *CPR 1272-81*, p.285.

27 *Ann. Dunstable*, p.279; *Ann. Waverley*, pp.390–1; *Wykes*, p.278; *Oxenedes*, p.252.
28 Zefira Entin Rokeah, 'Money and the hangman in late thirteenth-century England: Jews, Christians and coinage offences alleged and real: part 1', *JHS*, 31 (1988–90), pp.83–109, at pp.91, 96–7.
29 *CPR 1272–81*, p.338.
30 Hollister, *Henry I*, pp.297–8.
31 *Ann. Dunstable*, p.279; *Ann. London*, p.88; *Chron. Bury St. Edmunds*, p.67; *Wykes*, p.279.
32 Richardson, *English Jewry under Angevin Kings*, p.219.
33 Rokeah, 'Money and the hangman', p.98.
34 Ibid.
35 Ibid., pp.98–9.
36 *CCR 1272–9*, p.529.
37 Mundill, *England's Jewish Solution*, p.104.
38 For what follows here, see Brand, 'Jews and the Law', pp.1148–52.
39 Henry of Winchester's remarkable career is discussed by Stacey, 'Conversion of the Jews', pp.276–8.
40 Brand, 'Jews and the Law', p.1151.
41 Ibid., pp.1151–2.
42 Richardson, *English Jewry under Angevin Kings*, p.221 and n.1.
43 Ibid., pp.223–4; Brand, 'Jews and the Law', p.1151.
44 Prestwich, *Edward I*, pp.244–7.
45 Mundill, *England's Jewish Solution*, pp.106–7. The effects on York's Jews of the events of 1278–9 were certainly significant: Dobson, 'Decline and Expulsion', p.43.
46 *The London Eyre of 1276*, ed. Martin Weinbaum (London Record Society, 12, 1976), no.308; *CCR 1272–9*, pp.271–4; *Cotton*, p.159; *Oxenedes*, p.254.
47 *CPR 1272–81*, pp.287, 290.
48 For Robert of Reading, see above, pp.69–70.
49 *CPR 1272–81*, p.240.
50 *CCR 1272–9*, pp.565–6; *CCR 1279–88*, p.176. For Abraham, see *CPR 1272–81*, p.377; *Cal. Ch. R. 1257–1300*, p.213.
51 Chazan, *Church, State and Jew in the Middle Ages*, pp.255–63.
52 *CPR 1272–81*, p.356.
53 *CPR 1272–81*, pp.371–2.
54 Denholm-Young, *Richard of Cornwall*, pp.20, 69, 81 n.1, 143; Mundill, *England's Jewish Solution*, pp.60–2.
55 For a summary of Aaron's career, see Hillaby, 'London: the 13th-century Jewry revisited', pp.146–51. And see above, p.156.
56 *Ann. Waverley*, p.409; Howell, *Eleanor of Provence*, p.299.
57 *CPR 1272–81*, p.76; Howell, *Eleanor of Provence*, pp.263–4, 277.
58 *CPR 1272–81*, p.433.
59 Hillaby, 'London: the 13th-century Jewry revisited', pp.139–43; J.C. Parsons, *Eleanor of Castile. Queen and Society in Thirteenth Century England* (New York, 1995), pp.127, 144, 192.
60 'Le roy cuvayte nos deneres / e la reyne nos beau maners': *Guisborough*, p.216.
61 Parsons, *Eleanor of Castile*, pp.78–80, 138, 142, 312 n.49; Mundill, *England's Jewish Solution*, pp.62–3.
62 Stacey, 'Parliamentary negotiation', p.80.
63 Parsons, *Eleanor of Castile*, p.141.
64 *Registrum Epistolarum Fratris Johannis Peckham, Archiepiscopis Cantuariensis*, ed. C.T. Martin, 3 vols (RS, 1882–5), ii pp.619–20, 767–8, iii pp.937–8; Decima L. Douie, *Archbishop Pecham* (Oxford, 1952), p.328.

65   Mundill, *England's Jewish Solution*, p.273.
66   *Councils and Synods, II, 1205–1313*, ed. F.M. Powicke and C.R. Cheney, pp.959, 962;
      J.A. Watt, 'The English Episcopate, the State and the Jews: The Evidence of the
      Thirteenth-Century Conciliar Decrees', *TCE* II, p.144.
67   *Episcopal Registers of Richard de Swinfield Bishop of Hereford*, ed. W.W. Capes
      (Canterbury and York Society, 6, 1909), pp.120–1.
68   *Close Rolls 1268–72*, p.522; *Reg. Ep. Peckham*, i p.212–13, ii pp.407, 410–11; Hillaby,
      'London: the 13th-century Jewry revisited', pp.101, 149–51.
69   Prestwich, 'The piety of Edward I', in *England in the Thirteenth Century*, ed. W.M.
      Ormrod (Harlaxton, 1985), p.123; idem., *Edward I*, 112–13.
70   Stacey, 'Conversion of the Jews', p.267; Parsons, *Eleanor of Castile*, pp.57, 139–41;
      Howell, *Eleanor of Provence*, pp.90, 92–5
71   *CPREJ*, iii pp.311–12.
72   For the fullest development of this area, see Jeremy Cohen, *The Friars and the
      Jews: the Evolution of Medieval Anti-Judaism* (Ithaca, 1982).
73   *Calendar of Papal Registers, Papal Letters*, i, *1198–1304*, p.491; Roth, *History of the Jews*,
      p.77.
74   Stacey, 'Anti-Semitism and the medieval English State', pp.174–5.
75   Rigg, *Select Pleas*, pp.liv–lx; Brand, 'Jews and the Law', pp.1153–6; Stacey,
      'Parliamentary negotiation', pp.98–100; Mundill, *England's Jewish Solution*,
      pp.122–4.

6: Expulsion

1   Mundill, *England's Jewish Solution*, pp.25–7.
2   Roth, *History of the Jews*, p.79.
3   Above, p.121–2.
4   Mundill, *England's Jewish Solution*, Chapter 6 *passim*.
5   Above, p.122.
6   Mundill, *England's Jewish Solution*, p.208.
7   Ibid., pp.135–45. Brand restates the criticism: 'Jews and the Law', p.1153.
8   Above, p.122–3.
9   Dobson, 'Decline and Expulsion', pp.41–5.
10   Carpenter, *Struggle for Mastery*, p.488.
11   *Oxenedes*, p.268; *Wykes*, pp.308–9; *Ann. London*, p.96; *Chron. Bury St. Edmunds*,
      p.89; Prestwich, *Edward I*, p.344.
12   Prestwich, *Edward I*, p.345.
13   M. Prestwich, *War, Politics and Finance under Edward I* (London, 1972), pp.205–7;
      above, p.118.
14   R.W. Kaeuper, *Bankers to the Crown. The Riccardi of Lucca and Edward I* (Princeton,
      1973), pp.31–4; R.H. Bowers, 'From Rolls to Riches: King's Clerks and
      Moneylending in Thirteenth Century England', *Speculum*, 58 (1983), pp.60–71.
15   Richardson, *English Jewry under Angevin Kings*, p.108. For a contrary view,
      namely that 'the widening activities of the Italians is directly connected with the
      economic decline of the Jews', see Elman, 'The economic causes of the expulsion
      of the Jews in 1290', p.151.
16   Prestwich, *Edward I*, pp.323, 328.
17   There have been disagreements about the date of the Gascon expulsion. The
      modern consensus, that it took place at the end of 1287, is followed here:
      Mundill, *England's Jewish Solution*, p.276 and n.172.
18   Richardson, *English Jewry under Angevin Kings*, p.226.
19   For Edward I's relationship with Charles of Salerno, see Prestwich, *Edward I*,

pp.318–26; F.M. Powicke, *The Thirteenth Century* (Oxford, 1953), pp.251–64, 282–4.

20 Powicke, *The Thirteenth Century*, p.283.

21 Prestwich, *War, Politics and Finance under Edward I*, p.201. Prestwich made this statement believing that the expulsion was ordered and took place in 1289.

22 Mundill, *England's Jewish Solution*, pp.280–1.

23 Bartlett, *England under the Norman and Angevin Kings*, p.357.

24 *Jocelin of Brakelond*, pp.41–2; above, p.51.

25 For the Leicester expulsion, see above, pp.86, 105–6; for other references, see Mundill, *England's Jewish Solution*, p.265 n.88.

26 *CPR 1258–66*, p.153 (Derby), 613 (Romsey); *CCR 1272–9*, pp.50 (Winchelsea), 130 (Bridgnorth); *CPR 1272–81*, p.76.

27 Above, p.48; W.C. Jordan, *Louis IX and the Challenge of the Crusade*, pp.85–6; Chazan, *Church, State and Jew in the Middle Ages*, pp.310–13.

28 Mundill, *England's Jewish Solution*, pp.299–302; Chazan, *Church, State and Jew in the Middle Ages*, pp.313–17; idem., *Medieval Jewry in Northern France*, pp.184–6.

29 *CPR 1281–92*, p.318; Prestwich, *Edward I*, p.307.

30 *Wykes*, p.316.

31 Stacey, 'Parliamentary negotiation', p.83. For the 'state trials' of 1289–93, see Prestwich, *Edward I*, pp.339–42; Paul Brand, 'Edward I and the Judges: the 'State Trials of 1289–93', *TCE* I, pp.31–40; *State Trials in the Reign of Edward I, 1289–93*, ed. T.F. Tout and H. Johnstone (Camden Society, 3rd series, 9, 1906).

32 Prestwich, *Edward I*, p.342.

33 Stacey, 'Parliamentary negotiation', pp.84–5.

34 D.W. Sutherland, *Quo Warranto Proceedings in the Reign of Edward I, 1278–94* (Oxford, 1963), p.6.

35 Perhaps as many as 250 cases were still outstanding in 1290: Sutherland, *Quo Warranto*, pp.85–6.

36 *Rotuli Parliamentorum*, i (Record Commission, 1783), p.25; Stacey, 'Parliamentary negotiation', p.88; Prestwich, *Edward I*, pp.342–3

37 *CCR 1288–96*, pp.135–6.

38 For full references to them, see Stacey, 'Parliamentary negotiation', p.89, n.83.

39 Richardson, *English Jewry under Angevin Kings*, p.228; Mundill, *England's Jewish Solution*, p.253.

40 Stacey, 'Parliamentary negotiation', pp.89–90; Dobson, 'Decline and Expulsion', p.46; *CCR 1288–96*, p.91.

41 Stacey, 'Parliamentary negotiation', p.92.

42 *Guisborough*, pp.226–7; *Ann. Dunstable*, pp.361–2; *Ann. London*, p.99.

43 *CCR 1288–96*, pp.95–6; *Ann. Dunstable*, p.362.

44 Prestwich, *Edward I*, p.343; Stacey, 'Parliamentary negotiation', p.93.

45 *Ann. Dunstable*, p.362. For a different view, that the English Church was at best ambivalent about the expulsion of the Jews, see S. Menache, 'The King, the Church and the Jews: Some Considerations on the Expulsions from England and France', *Journal of Medieval History*, 13 (1987), pp.223–36.

46 *CCR 1288–96*, p.109.

47 Stacey, 'Jewish lending and the medieval English economy', p.100.

48 Mundill, *England's Jewish Solution*, pp.228–9, 233–4 and ch.7 *passim*.

49 David Stocker, 'The Shrine of Little St. Hugh', in *Medieval Art and Architecture at Lincoln Cathedral*, ed. T.A. Heslop and V. Sekules (Transactions of the British Archaeological Association Conference, 8 [1986], pp.109–17); Hillaby, 'The ritual child murder accusation', pp.95–8. Little of the original shrine now survives, but there is a drawing of it at ibid., p.97.

50 Hyams, 'Jewish Minority', p.288. For Jewish conversions under Edward I, see Stacey, 'Conversion of the Jews', pp.272–3.

51 *Ann. Waverley*, p.409; above, p.117, 133–4, 147; Howell, *Eleanor of Provence*, pp.300ff.
52 Elman, 'The economic causes of the expulsion of the Jews in 1290', p.152.
53 Watt, 'The English Episcopate, the State and the Jews', pp.146–7.
54 Richardson, *English Jewry under Angevin Kings*, p.231.
55 Roth, *History of the Jews*, p.86.
56 For Aaron and Cok, see above p.xxx.
57 *CPR 1281–92*, 378, 379, 382, 384; Dobson, 'Decline and Expulsion', p.46.
58 *Guisborough*, 226–7; Prestwich, *Edward I*, p.346; Roth, *History of the Jews*, pp.86–7.
59 *Cotton*, p.178; *Ann. Osney*, p.327; *CCR 1288–96*, p.295.
60 *CCR 1288–96*, p.109.
61 Abrahams, 'Condition of the Jews of England at the time of their Expulsion', p.85.
62 Mundill, *England's Jewish Solution*, pp.125–8, 256–7, 259.
63 *CPR 1281–92*, pp.410, 417.
64 *CCR 1288–96*, p.145.
65 They are transcribed in British Library, Lansdowne MS.826, fos.43–59, and outlined in *Rotulorum Originalium in Curia Scaccarii Abbreviatio Henry III – Edward III*, ed. H. Playford (London, 1805–10), i pp.73–6.
66 £956 6s 8d: Mundill, *England's Jewish Solution*, p.258. For a full list of the London properties, see Hillaby, 'London: the 13th-century Jewry revisited', pp.127, 152.
67 Mundill, *England's Jewish Solution*, p.258; Dobson, 'Decline and Expulsion', pp.46–8.
68 Mundill, *England's Jewish Solution*, p.259.
69 Ibid.; Roth, *The Jews of Medieval Oxford*, p.168; *The Oxford Deeds of Balliol College*, ed. H.E. Salter (Oxford Historical Society, 64, 1913), no.178.
70 Dobson, 'Decline and Expulsion', p.48; Mundill, *England's Jewish Solution*, pp.257–8.
71 Dobson, 'Decline and Expulsion', p.48; Richardson, *English Jewry under Angevin Kings*, p.230.
72 Mundill, *England's Jewish Solution*, p.259.
73 Richardson, *English Jewry under Angevin Kings*, p.230 and n.5.
74 Mundill, *England's Jewish Solution*, p.260.

7: Aftermath

1 Stacey, 'Conversion of the Jews', p.274 and refs.
2 Roth, *History of the Jews*, pp.133–4; Stacey, 'Conversion of the Jews', p.273.
3 Roth, *History of the Jews*, p.132.
4 Ibid., p.88; Chazan, *Medieval Jewry in Northern France*, pp.183–4. For the quotation about Bonamy, see Barrie Dobson, 'The Medieval York Jewry Reconsidered', in *Jews in Medieval Britain*, ed. Skinner, pp.145–56, at p.156 n.55.
5 Chazan, *Medieval Jewry in Northern France*, p.194.
6 Roth, *History of the Jews*, pp.87–8; Mundill, *England's Jewish Solution*, p.255.
7 Roth, *History of the Jews*, p.90.

Select Bibliography

This is not by any means an exhaustive list of relevant material. It includes those works which I have found most helpful in writing this book, and those which will give readers a deeper understanding of the events and issues I have discussed.

Unpublished Primary Sources

British Library, Lansdowne MS.826, fos.43–59

Printed Primary Sources

Annales Prioratus de Dunstaplia, A.D. 1–1377, in *Ann. Mon.*, iii
Annales Londonienses, Chronicles of the Reigns of Edward I and Edward II, i
Annales Monastici, ed. H.R. Luard, 5 vols (RS, 1864–9)
Annales Monasterii de Oseneia, 1016–1347, in *Ann. Mon.*, iv
Annales Monasterii de Waverleia, A.D. 1–1291, in *Ann. Mon.*, ii
Bartholomaei de Cotton, Historia Anglicana (A.D. 449–1298), ed. H.R. Luard (RS, 1859)
Calendar of Charter Rolls (London, 1916–)
Calendar of Close Rolls (London, 1903–)
Calendar of Papal Registers, Papal Letters, i, 1198–1304 (London, 1893)
Calendar of Patent Rolls (London, 1906–)
Calendar of the Plea Rolls of the Exchequer of the Jews, ed. J.M. Rigg and others, 5 vols (Jewish Historical Society of England, 1905–792)
Chronica Johannis de Oxenedes, ed. H. Ellis (RS, 1859)

Chronica Magistri Rogeri de Hovedene, ed. W. Stubbs, 4 vols (RS, 1868–71)

The Chronicle of Bury St. Edmunds, 1212–1301, ed. A. Gransden (London, 1964)

The Chronicle of Walter of Guisborough, ed. H. Rothwell (Camden Society, 1957)

The Chronicles of the Reigns of Henry II and Richard I, A.D.1169–92, ed. W. Stubbs, 2 vols (RS, 1867)

Chronicles of the Reigns of Stephen, Henry I and Richard I, ed. R. Howlett, 4 vols (RS, 1885–90)

Chronicon vulgo dicitur Chronicon Thomae Wykes, 1066–1289, in *Ann. Mon.*, iv

Close Rolls of the Reign of Henry III (London, 1902–)

Councils and Synods, II, 1205–1313, ed. F.M. Powicke and C.R. Cheney (Oxford, 1964)

Curia Regis Rolls (London, 1922–)

De Antiquis Legibus Liber. Cronica Maiorum et Vicecomitum Londiniarum, ed. T. Stapleton (Camden Society, 1846)

Dialogus de Scaccario and Constitutio Domus Regis, ed. C. Johnson (revised edn, Oxford, 1983)

Documents of the Baronial Movement of Reform and Rebellion, 1258–67, ed. R.F. Treharne and I.J. Sanders (Oxford, 1973)

The Early Rolls of Merton College, ed. J.R.L. Highfield (Oxford Historical Society, new series, 18, 1964)

English Historical Documents, II, 1042–1189, ed. D.C. Douglas and G.W. Greenaway (London, 2nd edn, 1981)

English Historical Documents, III, 1189–1327, ed. H. Rothwell (London, 1975)

English Lawsuits from William I to Richard I, ed. R.C. Van Caenegem, 2 vols (Selden Society, 1990–91)

Episcopal Registers of Richard de Swinfield Bishop of Hereford, ed. W.W. Capes (Canterbury and York Society, 6, 1909)

Excerpta e Rotulis Finium in Turri Londiniensi Asservatis … AD 1216-72, ed. C. Roberts, 2 vols (Record Commission, 1835–6)

'Extracts from the Close Rolls, 1279–1288', ed. A. Corcos, *TJHSE*, 4 (1903)

'Extracts from the Close Rolls, 1289–1368', ed. H.P. Stokes, *TJHSE*, Miscellanies, 1 (1925)

Flores Historiarum, ed. H.R. Luard, 3 vols (RS, 1890)

Foedera, Conventiones, Litterae, et Acta Publica, ed. T. Rymer, 4 vols (Record Commission, 1816)

Gerald of Wales. The Journey through Wales and the Description of Wales, trans. Lewis Thorpe (London, 1978)

The Historical Works of Gervase of Canterbury, ed. W. Stubbs, 2 vols (RS, 1879–80)

'The Jewish entries from the Patent Rolls, 1272–92', ed. R. Mundill, *JHS*, 32 (1993)

The Jews and the Crusaders. The Hebrew Chronicles of the First and Second Crusades, trans. and ed. Shlomo Eidelberg (Madison, 1977)

Jocelin of Brakelond. Chronicle of the Abbey of Bury St Edmunds, trans. Diana Greenway and Jane Sayers (Oxford, 1989)

The Life and Miracles of St. William of Norwich, by Thomas of Monmouth, ed. A. Jessopp and M.R. James (Cambridge, 1896)

The London Eyre of 1276, ed. Martin Weinbaum (London Record Society, 12, 1976)

Materials for the History of Thomas Becket, Archbishop of Canterbury, ed. J.C. Robertson, 7 vols (RS, 1875–85)

Matthaei Parisiensis Historia Anglorum sive ut Vulgo Dicitur Historia Minor (1067-1253), ed. F. Madden, 3 vols (RS, 1866–9)

Matthaei Parisiensis Monachi Sancti Albani Chronica Majora, ed. H.R. Luard, 7 vols (RS, London, 1872–84)

Medieval English Jews and Royal Officials: Entries of Jewish Interest in the English Memoranda Rolls, 1266–1293, ed. Zefira Entin Rokeah (Jerusalem, 2000)

Nicholai Triveti Annales, ed. T. Hog (London, 1845)

The Oxford Deeds of Balliol College, ed. H.E. Salter (Oxford Historical Society, 64, 1913)

The Pipe Roll of 31 Henry I, ed. J. Hunter (London, 1929)

Radulphi de Coggeshall Chronicon Anglicanum, ed. J. Stevenson (RS, 1875)

Registrum Epistolarum Fratris Johannis Peckham, Archiepiscopis Cantuariensis, ed. C.T. Martin, 3 vols (RS, 1882–5)

Rotulorum Originalium in Curia Scaccarii Abbreviatio Henry III-Edward III, ed. H. Playford (London, 1805–10)

Rotuli Chartarum in Turri Londinensi aservati, 1199–1216, ed. T. Duffus Hardy (Record Commission, 1837)

Rotuli Litterarum Clausarum in Turri Londinensi asservati, ed. T. Duffus Hardy (Record Commission, 1833–4)

Rotuli Litterarum Patentium in Turri Londinensi asservati, ed. T. Duffus Hardy (Record Commission, 1835)

Rotuli de Oblatis et Finibus in Turri Londinensi asservati, ed. T. Duffus Hardy (Record Commission, 1835)

Rotuli Parliamentorum, i (Record Commission, 1783)

Royal and other Historical Letters illustrative of the Reign of Henry III, ed. W.W. Shirley, 2 vols (RS, 1862–6)

Select Pleas, Starrs and other Records from the Rolls of the Exchequer of the Jews (1220-1284), ed. J. M. Rigg (Selden Society, 15, 1901–2)

Self and Society in Medieval France, ed. J. Benton (New York, 1970)

State Trials in the Reign of Edward I, 1289–93, ed. T.F. Tout and H. Johnstone (Camden Society, 3rd series, 9, 1906)

Tractatus de legibus et consuetudines regni Anglie qui Glanvilla vocatur, ed. G.D.G. Hall (Oxford, 1965)

William of Malmesbury, Gesta Regum Anglorum, ed. and trans. R.A.B. Mynors; completed by R.M. Thomson and M. Winterbottom, 2 vols (Oxford and New York, 1998)

Secondary Works

Abrahams, B. Lionel, 'The Condition of the Jews at the Time of their Expulsion in 1290', *TJHSE*, 2 (1894–5)

Abrahams, I., 'The Northampton "Donum" of 1194', *TJHSE*, Miscellanies, 1 (1925)

Adler, M., *The Jews of Medieval England* (London, 1939)

Asbridge, T., *The First Crusade. A New History* (London, 2004)

Barratt, N., 'The Revenue of King John', *EHR*, 111 (1996)

Bartlet, Suzanne, 'Three Jewish Businesswomen in Thirteenth-Century Winchester', *Jewish Culture and History*, vol. 3 no. 2 (Winter, 2000)

—, 'Women in the Medieval Anglo-Jewish Community', in *Jews in Medieval Britain*, ed. Skinner

Bartlett, Robert, *The Making of Europe* (London, 1993)

—, *England under the Norman and Angevin Kings, 1075–1225* (Oxford, 2000)

The Blackwell Encyclopaedia of Anglo-Saxon England, ed. Michael Lapidge, John Blair, Simon Keynes and Donald Scragg (Oxford, 1999)

Bowers, R.H., 'From Rolls to Riches: King's Clerks and Moneylending in Thirteenth Century England', *Speculum*, 58 (1983)

Brand, Paul, 'Edward I and the Judges: the 'State Trials of 1289–93', *TCE* I (1986)

—, 'Jews and the Law in England, 1275–90', *EHR*, 115 (2000)

—, 'The Jewish Community in the Records of Royal Government', in *Jews in Medieval Britain*, ed. Skinner

Britnell, R.H., *Britain and Ireland 1050–1530. Economy and Society* (Oxford, 2004)

Brown, R. Berman and McCartney, S., 'David of Oxford and Licoricia of Winchester: glimpses into a Jewish family in thirteenth-century England', *JHS*, 39 (2004)

Campbell, J., 'The Late Anglo-Saxon State: a Maximum View', *Proceedings of the British Academy*, 87 (1994), repr. in idem., *The Anglo–Saxon State* (London, 2000)

Carpenter, D.A., *The Minority of Henry III* (London, 1990)

—, *The Struggle for Mastery. Britain, 1066–1284* (London, 2003)

Chazan, Robert, '1007–1012: Initial Crisis for North-European Jewry', *Proceedings of the American Academy for Jewish Research*, 38–9 (1970–71)

—, *Medieval Jewry in Northern France* (Baltimore, 1973)

—, *Church, State and Jew in the Middle Ages* (West Orange, N.J., 1980)

—, *European Jewry and the First Crusade* (London, 1987)

Cluse, C., 'Stories of breaking and taking the cross: a possible context for the Oxford incident of 1268', *Revue d'histoire ecclésiastique*, 90 (1995)

Cohen, Jeremy, *The Friars and the Jews: the Evolution of Medieval Anti-Judaism* (Ithaca, 1982)

A Commercialising Economy. England, 1086-1300, ed. R.H. Britnell and B.M.S. Campbell (Manchester, 1995)

Coss, Peter, *The Origins of the English Gentry* (Cambridge, 2003)

Denholm-Young, N., *Richard of Cornwall* (Oxford, 1947)

De Ville, Oscar, entry on 'Deyville, Sir John de', in *ODNB*

Dobson, R.B. *The Jews of Medieval York and the Massacre of March 1190* (Borthwick Papers, no.45, York, 1974)

—, 'The Decline and Expulsion of the Medieval Jews of York', *TJHSE* 26 (1979)

—, 'The role of Jewish Women in Medieval England', in *Christianity and Judaism*, ed. D. Wood (*Studies in Church History*, 29, Oxford, 1992)

—, 'The Medieval York Jewry Reconsidered', in *Jews in Medieval Britain*, ed. Skinner

Douie, Decima L., *Archbishop Pecham* (Oxford, 1952)

Elman, Peter, 'The economic causes of the expulsion of the Jews in 1290', *Economic History Review*, 7 (1936–7)

Green, Judith, *The Government of England under Henry I* (Cambridge, 1986)

Hillaby, Joe, 'A magnate among the marchers: Hamo of Hereford, his family and his clients, 1218–1253', *JHS*, 31 (1988–90)

—, 'The Hereford Jewry 1179–1290 – Aaron le Blund and the last decades of Hereford Jewry 1253–1290', *Transactions of the Woolhope Naturalists Field Club*, 46(3) (1990)

—, 'London: the 13th-century Jewry Revisited', *JHS*, 32 (1990–92)

—, 'Beth Miqdash Me-at: the synagogues of medieval England', *Journal of Ecclesiastical*

History, 44 (1991)

—, 'The London Jewry: William I to John', *JHS*, 33 (1992–1994)

—, 'The ritual child murder accusation: its dissemination and Harold of Gloucester', *JHS*, 34 (1994–6)

—, 'Jewish Colonisation in the Twelfth Century', in *Jews in Medieval Britain*, ed. Skinner

Hollister, C.W., *Henry I* (Yale, 2001)

Holt, J.C., *The Northerners* (Oxford, 1961)

—, *Magna Carta* (2nd edn, Cambridge, 1992)

Honeybourne, M.B., 'The pre-expulsion cemetery of the Jews in London', *TJHSE*, 20 (1959–61)

Howell, Margaret, *Eleanor of Provence* (Oxford, 1998)

Hyams, Paul, 'The Jewish Minority in Medieval England, 1066–1290', *JJS*, 25 (1974)

Jenkinson, H., 'William Cade, a financier of the twelfth century', *EHR*, 28 (1913)

The Jewish Heritage in British History: Englishness and Jewishness, ed. Tony Kushner (London, 1992)

Jews in Medieval Britain. Historical, Literary and Archaeological Perspectives, ed. Patricia Skinner (Woodbridge, 2003)

Jordan, W.C., *Louis IX and the Challenge of the Crusade* (Princeton, 1979)

Kaeuper, R.W., *Bankers to the Crown. The Riccardi of Lucca and Edward I* (Princeton, 1973)

King, Edmund, entry on 'Cade, William', in *ODNB*

Langmuir, Gavin I., 'The Knight's Tale of Young Hugh of Lincoln', *Speculum*, 47 (1972)

—, 'Thomas of Monmouth: Detector of Ritual Murder', *Speculum*, 59 (1984)

Lipman, Vivian D., *The Jews of Medieval Norwich* (London, 1967)

—, 'Anatomy of Medieval Anglo-Jewry', *TJHSE*, 21 (1968)

Maddicott, J.R., 'The Crusade Taxation of 1268–70 and the Development of Parliament', *TCE* II (1988)

—, *Simon de Montfort* (London, 1994)

Mayhew, Nicholas, 'Modelling medieval monetisation', in *A commercialising economy. England, 1086 to c.1300*, ed. Britnell and Campbell

McComish, Jane, 'The Medieval Jewish Cemetery at Jewbury, York', *Jewish Culture and History*, vol. 3 no. 2 (Winter, 2000)

McCulloh, John, 'Jewish ritual murder: William of Norwich, Thomas of Monmouth and the early dissemination of the myth', *Speculum*, 72 (1997)

The Medieval State: Essays Presented to James Campbell, ed. J.R. Maddicott and D.M. Palliser (London, 2000)

Menache, S., 'The King, the Church and the Jews: Some Considerations on the Expulsions from England and France', *Journal of Medieval History*, 13 (1987)

Mundill, Robin R., *England's Jewish Solution. Experiment and Expulsion, 1262–1290* (Cambridge, 1998)

O'Brien, Bruce R., *God's Peace and King's Peace: the Laws of Edward the Confessor* (Philadelphia, 1999)

Oxford Dictionary of National Biography, in association with the British Academy. From the earliest times to the year 2000, ed. H.C.G. Matthew and Brian Harrison (Oxford, 2004)

Parsons, J.C., *Eleanor of Castile. Queen and Society in Thirteenth Century England* (New York, 1995)

Powicke, F.M., *King Henry III and the Lord Edward*, 2 vols (Oxford, 1947)

—, *The Thirteenth Century* (Oxford, 1953)

Prestwich, M., *War, Politics and Finance under Edward I* (London, 1972)

—, 'The piety of Edward I', in *England in the Thirteenth Century*, ed. W.M. Ormrod (Harlaxton, 1985)

—, *Edward I* (Yale, 1997)

Richardson, H.G., *The English Jewry under Angevin Kings* (London, 1960)

Richmond, Colin, 'Englishness and Medieval Anglo-Jewry', in *The Jewish Heritage in British History*, ed. Kushner

Rokeah, Zefirah Entin, 'Money and the hangman in late thirteenth-century England: Jews, Christians and coinage offences alleged and real: part 1', *JHS*, 31 (1988–90)

Roth, Cecil, *The Jews of Medieval Oxford* (Oxford Historical Society, new series, 9, 1945–6)

—, 'A day in the life of a medieval English Jew', in idem., *Essays and Portraits in Anglo-Jewish History* (London and Philadelphia, 1962)

—, *History of the Jews in England* (3rd edn, Oxford, 1964)

—, 'Why Anglo-Jewish history?' *TJHSE*, 22 (1968–9)

Stacey, Robert C., *Politics, Policy and Finance under Henry III* (Oxford, 1987)

—, '1240-60: a Watershed in Anglo-Jewish Relations?', *Bulletin of the Institute of Historical Research*, 61 (1988)

—, 'The Conversion of Jews to Christianity in thirteenth-century England', *Speculum*, 67 (1992)

—, 'Parliamentary negotiation and the Expulsion of the Jews from England', *TCE* VI (1997)

—, 'Anti-Semitism and the medieval English state', in *The Medieval State*, ed. Maddicott and Palliser

—, 'Jewish lending and the medieval English economy', in *A commercialising economy. England, 1086 to c.1300*, ed. Britnell and Campbell

—, 'The English Jews under Henry III', in *Jews in Medieval Britain*, ed. Skinner

—, entries on 'Eveske, Elias l", 'Lexinton, John of', 'Lincoln, Aaron of', 'Norwich, Isaac of', 'York, Aaron of', in *ODNB*

Stocker, David, 'The Shrine of Little St. Hugh', in *Medieval Art and Architecture at Lincoln Cathedral*, ed. T.A. Heslop and V. Sekules (Transactions of the British Archaeological Association Conference, 8, [1986])

Streit, K.T., 'The expansion of the Jewish community in the reign of King Stephen', *Albion*, 25 (1993)

Sutherland, D.W., *Quo Warranto Proceedings in the Reign of Edward I, 1278–94* (Oxford, 1963)

Thirteenth Century England: Proceedings of the Newcastle-Upon-Tyne and Durham Conferences, ed. P.R. Coss and others (Woodbridge, 1986–)

Vincent, Nicholas, 'Two papal letters on the wearing of the Jewish badge, 1221 and 1239', *JHS*, 34 (1994–6)

Watt, J.A., 'The English Episcopate, the State and the Jews: The Evidence of the Thirteenth-Century Conciliar Decrees', *TCE* II (1988)

Yuval, Israel Jacob, '"Vengeance and damnation, blood and defamation": from Jewish martyrdom to blood libel accusations', *Zion*, 58 (1993)

List of Illustrations

Index

TEMPUS — REVEALING HISTORY

The Wars of the Roses
The Soldiers' Experience
ANTHONY GOODMAN
'Sheds light on the lot of the common soldier as never before' *Alison Weir*
£25
0 7524 1784 3

The Vikings
MAGNUS MAGUNSSON
'Serious, engaging history'
BBC History Magazine
£9.99
0 7524 2699 0

 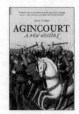

William the Conqueror
DAVID BATES
'As expertly woven as the Bayeux Tapestry'
BBC History Magazine
£12.99
0 7524 2960 4

Agincourt: A New History
ANNE CURRY
'Overturns a host of assumptions about this most famous of English victories... *the* book on the battle' *Richard Holmes*
£25
0 7524 2828 4

Hereward The Last Englishman
PETER REX
'An enthralling work of historical detection' *Robert Lacey*
£17.99
0 7524 3318 0

The English Resistance
The Underground War Against the Normans
PETER REX
'An invaluable rehabilitation of an ignored resistance movement' ***The Sunday Times***
£17.99
0 7524 2827 6

Richard III
MICHAEL HICKS
'A most important book by the greatest living expert on Richard' *Desmond Seward*
£9.99
0 7524 2589 7

The Peasants Revolt
England's Failed Revolution of 1381
ALASTAIR DUNN
'A stunningly good book... totally absorbing' *Melvyn Bragg*
£9.99
0 7524 2965 5

If you are interested in purchasing other books published by Tempus, or in case you have difficulty finding any Tempus books in your local bookshop, you can also place orders directly through our website:
www.tempus-publishing.com